FALCON STYLE GUIDE
A Comprehensive Guide
for Travel and Outdoor
Writers and Editors

Erica S. Olsen

FALCON®
HELENA, MONTANA

Text pages printed on recycled paper.

Foreword

We think that this may be the only style guide you'll ever use that includes the word *frontcountry*. No, we didn't make it up—nor did we invent *armbar, chickenhead,* or *kelly hump.* Words like these, and issues such as number style, naming roads, and whether a fisher is a member of the weasel family or another nonsexist term for an angler, plague the outdoor writer and her editor on a daily basis.

After years of editorial meetings filled with hot debates over the use of "switchback" as a verb (try to find that in the *American Heritage Dictionary* or the *Chicago Manual of Style*), we rejoiced when fine freelance proofreader Erica Olsen volunteered her services to us as author of the definitive *Falcon Style Guide,* compiling years of notes, style sheets, and previous style guides by the Falcon staff. Before her gargantuan effort to bring elements of the outdoor and travel world together in this beautifully organized guide to writing about both, no single source covered or even included most of the terms and issues discussed here.

Topics included in this book cover everything from fishing lures to historical figures to tips for writing directions. In addition, several helpful appendixes list federal, state, and local agencies, national parks, and tribal names. But this guide is not just a primer on style for outdoor and travel writers. The discussions of punctuation and usage will help any writer find his way through complex sentences and into a clearer, more precise prose.

We at Falcon Publishing and its imprints—FalconGuides, TwoDot, The Insiders' Guides, Chockstone Press, and ThreeForks—look forward to many productive years with this style guide on our desks.

The Falcon, Chockstone, TwoDot, ThreeForks, and Insiders' staffs.

About Falcon Publishing and Its Imprints

Falcon Publishing, Inc., is a division of Landmark Communications, a Virginia Corporation. Until 1997 Falcon was independently owned and operated in Helena, Montana, where the offices are located. Falcon produces approximately 100 new titles a year in all of its divisions. In addition to the titles listed below, Falcon also produces photo gift books, calendars, and titles on nature and conservation.

FalconGuides—This is Falcon's flagship imprint with titles on hiking, mountain biking, camping, paddling, fishing, wildlife watching, walking, trail riding, rockhounding, scenic driving, hot springs, and skiing. In addition to books that tell you where to pursue your favorite activities, how-to books on topics such as backpacking and using GPS are a popular series. Wildflower field guides and other field guides round out the offerings.

TwoDot—TwoDot books is Falcon Publishing's history imprint. In addition to series such as "It Happened in" and "More than Petticoats," this imprint produces high-quality one-of-a-kind books on fascinating topics in American history for a general audience.

Chockstone Press—If you want to go rock climbing, read about rock climbing, or learn how to rock climb, Chockstone Press has the books for you, with both regional and state-specific guidebooks on where to go, technical titles, and essay and fiction on this popular sport.

Insiders' Guides—This series of guidebooks takes you to cities and regions all over the United States with hotel and restaurant reviews, area attractions, and superb relocation information.

ThreeForks—Falcon's cookbook imprint offers regional and national cookbooks with a wide range of themes and appeal.

Contents

Preface

Is *spray skirt* one word or two? What is a *national natural landmark*? Should *tribe* be capitalized when referring to the *Hopi Tribe*? Is there a hyphen in *field-dressed*? *The Falcon Style Guide* has the answers to all of these questions and many more. The first truly comprehensive manual of style for outdoor and travel writing, this book offers detailed treatment of topics not covered by the *Chicago Manual of Style* and the *AP Stylebook*.

In Falcon's nearly 25-year history, its editors have developed a writing and editing style that is clear and useful for authors, copy editors, proofreaders, and indexers of outdoor-related publications. The *Style Guide* summarizes this style. It has been organized with the outdoor writer or editor in mind. An A-to-Z format makes information available at a glance. Style decisions that would previously have had to be deduced from the *Chicago* rules are indexed in an intuitive manner and illustrated with examples and exceptions. Expert editors, as well as people who have never picked up a style guide before, can use this book. It will be useful to other publishers that emphasize outdoor-related materials and to natural resource agencies, environmental groups, and students.

The *Style Guide* has a threefold purpose. First, it presents some of the most basic style rules—such as capitalization of place names, compounding, and hyphenation—together with a wide range of examples. Second, it provides guidelines for achieving a consistent style in handling topics such as conservation and administrative designations and more complex place names. As with any style guide, users are free to accept or reject individual points, but our approach should give you confidence that you are making correct, consistent decisions.

Third, this is a handbook of information on names and terminology frequently encountered in writing about the outdoors. This aspect of the book is not limited to trademarks and sports jargon, but includes entries on the arts, historical figures and events, and scientific terms. Some of these are provided mainly because they are frequently misspelled, but most are glossed or annotated to clarify their context. Thus, the book is a valuable reference for working editors and proofreaders who may be unfamiliar with particular subjects in outdoor-related writing. We think it is the only book in which terms such as *Concord coach, transcontinental railroad,* and *Corps of Topographical Engineers* appear along with *Biosphere Reserve* and *National Champion Tree, snowmachine* and *snowcat, leks* and *pocosin,* and *Petzl Grigri* and *Polartec.*

If you work with guidebooks, field guides, or any other kind of writing about the outdoors, please send your comments, suggestions, and, of course, corrections or refinements to

> Style Guide
> Falcon Publishing
> P.O. Box 1718
> Helena, MT 59624

How to
use this book

The overview offers a thematic treatment of topics covered in individual A-to-Z entries. Various style decisions are discussed in relation to each other, so you can understand the approach to consistency and make your own decisions about issues that are not covered in this book.

The main section of the book is organized in dictionary style. Examples are shown in italics. Many compounds are indexed by root, so that you can look up *cheatgrass* directly, or look under *grass* to find the pattern of compounds that include the word *grass*. Animal names are listed in the following order: singular, plural, male, female, young.

Falcon relies on the *American Heritage Dictionary* and the *Chicago Manual of Style*, 14th ed., as its primary references. In some cases, rules presented in this style guide contradict those sources.

What this book does not include

We have omitted discussion of how to handle notes and bibliography, which is readily available in *Chicago*. Also, this book is meant as a reference for writing directed at a general audience, not scholarly work in the natural sciences.

Overview

Abbreviations and Acronyms

acronyms

Do not use periods for letter abbreviations of organizations and government agencies: *NOLS,* not *N.O.L.S.,* for the *National Outdoor Leadership School.* (Exception: Use periods if the organization itself requires periods.)

addresses

Spell out terms for roads in text: *Higgins Avenue,* not *Higgins Ave.;* the *Beartooth Highway,* not the *Beartooth Hwy.* Also spell out directional terms: *West Crosby Street.* For numbered streets, spell out numbers from one to ten, and use numerals for numbers above ten: *West First Street, 46th Avenue.*

degrees

B.A., M.D., M.F.A., Ph.D., but *a master's degree*

initials

Put a space between the initials in a person's name: *E. B. White.* A line break should never fall between the initials.

measurement

Spell out terms of measurement in text: a *300-pound bear,* not a *300-lb. bear.* The tree is *100 feet high,* not *100 ft.* or *100´ high.*

Okay to abbreviate rates such as cfs (cubic feet per second) when there are many such figures mentioned.

Also see **Numbers,** p. 27.

P.O. Box

No space between the letters *P.O.*

state names

Write out all state names that appear in the body of the text: *Montana*, not *Mont.* or *MT*. Thus: Falcon Publishing, P.O. Box 1718, Helena, Montana 59624.

When the state name follows a city, but is not part of a full address, set off the state name with commas: Early risers sometimes see elk in the streets of *Missoula, Montana*, just before dawn.

Use two-letter postal abbreviations for state names when listing an address in multicolumn or appendix format. Thus, in a list:

> Falcon Publishing, Inc.
> P.O. Box 1718
> Helena, MT 59624

titles

Abbreviate *Mr., Mrs., Ms., Dr.* before a name. Write out military titles. Write out a title used alone in speech: *"Doctor,* can you help me?"

Compounds and Hyphenation

Some compounds have standard forms: two-word, open compounds *(dirt road)*; hyphenated compounds *(black-and-white)*; one-word compounds *(grasslands)*. See individual entries for such terms. For an excellent analysis of kinds of compounds, see the *Government Printing Office Style Manual.*

In writing about the outdoors, note the following situations:

animal names

Typical form: *white-tailed deer* (but *whitetail*), *ruby-throated hummingbird.*

avoid ambiguity

Use a hyphen to link modifiers whose connection may not be immediately apparent, as when the first term encountered is a noun: *a trail-weary hiker.*

best

Hyphenate a compound adjective with *best* before a noun: one of the *best-known* places. No hyphen after the noun: This lake is *best known* for trout.

colors

Hyphenate if the colors are of equal value: *blue-green algae.* No hyphen if one color modifies another: *bluish green paint.*

directions

northwest, but *north-northwest*

-ed compounds

Hyphenate before a noun: *a well-equipped hiker.* No hyphen necessary after the noun: *That hiker is well equipped.*

-ing compounds (noun plus gerund)

When the word ending in *-ing* is a gerund (a verb used as a noun), do not hyphenate: *rock climbing, ice fishing, snow camping.* No hyphen if such a term modifies another term, as long as no ambiguity results: *a rock climbing guidebook.*

-ing compounds (noun plus present participle)

When the word ending in *-ing* is a present participle, hyphenate the compound before a noun, but not after: *a crowd-pleasing show.*

letters

Hyphenate combinations of letters plus the word *shaped: a U-shaped valley.* Use a sans serif font for *U-shaped* and *V-shaped.*

See individual entries for compound nouns in which one element is a capital letter. These are usually, but not always, hyphenated: *T-shirt, U-lock,* but *J stroke.*

-ly adverb plus verb

No hyphen required: *federally managed land*. The adverb already modifies the verb, so there is no need to link the terms further.

measurement

Hyphenate a number plus a unit of measurement when the term precedes a noun: *a 10-foot pole, a 5-mile hike*. No hyphen after the noun: *I hiked 5 miles before breakfast*. Avoid the common error of adding a hyphen between the term of measurement and the noun: never *a two-hour-hike*.

plant names

Plant names that include the terms *berry, brush, grass, weed*, and *wort* tend to be written as closed compounds: *huckleberry, rabbitbrush, bluegrass, tumbleweed, sandwort*.

prefixes and suffixes

Words beginning with a prefix such as *non, re, un* are usually written as one word, as are words ending in a suffix such as *like* or *most*. See individual entries for further discussion and examples. For readability, it is sometimes desirable to separate two vowels with a hyphen: *anti-inflammatory*, not *antiinflammatory*. It is always acceptable to hyphenate if the resulting compound is hard to read or suggests an incorrect meaning.

proper nouns

No hyphen in terms like *a Two Grey Hills rug* or *a National Park Service publication*.

verbs

No hyphen in phrasal verbs such as to *follow up, listen in*, or *work out*. Noun forms may be one word (*backup*) or hyphenated (*break-in*). See individual entries or consult a dictionary.

water

Two words when the first term simply describes the second: *cold water, warm water, fresh water, salt water*. One word when describing habitat: *freshwater, coldwater*. The adjective form is usually one word: *saltwater, freshwater, bluewater, coldwater.*

well

Compounds with *well* are hyphenated before the noun, but not after: *Those animals are well camouflaged,* but *well-camouflaged animals are hard to see.*

Grammar, Punctuation, and Typography

apostrophe

Apostrophes do not generally appear in U.S. place names, although they were often present in the original form of names and occasionally may persist in local usage. There is no apostrophe today in names such as *Devils Tower* or *Pikes Peak,* but an apostrophe may appear in historical references, such as titles of older books and quotations of original sources. *Martha's Vineyard* is a rare place name that does have an apostrophe.

Apostrophes often do not appear in names that look as if they are possessives: *Idaho Outfitters and Guides Association.* In this example, "Outfitters and Guides" is attributive, modifying "Association." A similar construction is seen in the term "citizens band," which also has no apostrophe. Such names should be verified, however, since some groups do use an apostrophe.

Also see **Plurals** and **Possessives.**

colon

This punctuation mark is always preceded by a complete main clause. A colon can be used to introduce a formal statement, an extract, a subtitle, speech in dialogue, a list, or a series. Never use a colon to introduce a list that is a complement or object of an element in the introductory statement: "The three bears had porridge, beds, and chairs," not "The three bears had: porridge, beds, and chairs."

Capitalize the first word after a colon if the phrase before the colon is a heading or a title, as in "Bear Aware: Hiking and Camping in Bear Country" or "General description: This is a short, easy hike."

Do not capitalize the first word after a colon in text, unless what follows is a formal announcement or more than one sentence.

Also see **Semicolon.**

comma

Use a comma before the last item in a series: *red, white, and blue.* Maps of *California, Wyoming,* and *Nevada.* Exception: in names of organizations and agencies, follow their preferred style.

Do not use commas to set off a restrictive phrase or clause, which contains information that could not be dropped from the sentence: *The campers with smoked salmon in their tent worried about bears all night long.*

Use commas to set off descriptive phrases and nonrestrictive phrases and clauses. Right: *Jean and Bob, who were fast asleep in their tent, had no idea the bear was approaching.* Wrong: *Jean and Bob who were fast asleep in their tent had no idea the bear was approaching.*

Do not use a comma to separate a long compound subject from its verb. Right: *Two rangers, an archaeologist, and several volunteers have been visiting the site.* Wrong: *Two rangers, an archaeologist, and several volunteers, have been visiting the site.*

With numbers: Use a comma to mark the thousands place: *1,500 deer; 30,000 years.* With dates: *1998, 1500 B.C.,* but *15,000 B.C.* No commas in street address numbers *(10515 Los Angeles Avenue)*, broadcast frequencies *(1250 AM)*, or fraternal or labor organizations *(Local 1101)*.

dashes

em dash

An em dash (—) is the longest dash typically used. It is used to denote sudden changes, to introduce a phrase that amplifies, explains, or digresses from the main clause, or to set off a complementary element in a sentence (a job that can also be done by commas or parentheses). There is no additional letter space between the words on either side of an em dash.

The em dash is less formal than a colon or a semicolon. Overuse should be avoided.

en dash

An en dash (–) is shorter than an em dash and longer than a hyphen. Its main function is to connect continuing or inclusive numbers, such as dates, time, or page numbers. *May–July 1997, 1997–1998, 8–11 A.M., Helena–Spokane flight, pages 14–20.* In running text (except in cookbooks or tabular material), use of the word *to* is preferable: *May to July 1997, 8 to 11 A.M., Helena to Spokane flight.*

The en dash is also used in text to connect terms in a compound adjective, when one or both of the terms is itself a compound or hyphenated term. *a Civil War–era gun.*

hyphens

Use a hyphen to connect simple compounds, in which one word is connected to another (as in many animal names): *red-winged blackbird.* For guidelines on hyphenation and compounding, see page 5.

Also see **Dashes.**

italics

A punctuation mark that follows an italicized word should also be italicized. She traveled with copies of *Desert Solitaire, The Monkey Wrench Gang,* and *Walden.*

If all of the words within parentheses are italicized, italicize the parentheses: She brought her favorite book *(Desert Solitaire)* along on her trip. If an italicized word is adjacent to only one of the parentheses, leave the parentheses in roman type: She packed a few favorite possessions (including her lucky bandanna and a copy of *Desert Solitaire*). The same rule applies to quotation marks.

Use roman type for a possessive *'s* after an italicized word: "*Outside*'s September issue." Less unwieldy, though, is "the September issue of *Outside*." For plural, add a roman "s": two *Outside*s.

plurals

To form the plural of a letter abbreviation, add a lowercase "s": YMCAs, RURPs, 1900s, Ps and Qs.

Form the plural with *'s* only for abbreviations with periods and abbreviations that end in the letter "s" or that would otherwise be hard to read: M.D.'s, SOS's.

For plurals of animal names, see individual entries. Singular terms are often used instead of plurals to indicate representatives of a species: *Black bear, beaver, and moose can all be seen in this area*. Let your ear be the guide in such cases. Use the standard plural form when referring to a specific number of individual animals: *Bears have been coming close to the house. Look, there are two beavers.*

possessives

Form the possessives of all singular nouns, no matter what letter they end with, by adding *'s*: *Charles's tent, Jane's rope, Minneapolis's parks, Billings's airport*. Infelicities can often be avoided by rewording: *the parks of Minneapolis*.

Form the possessives of plural nouns by adding a simple apostrophe: *the rangers' radios, the campers' tents*.

Rephrase to avoid the awkward possessives formed by adding *'s* to a long compound noun: *the museum at the park visitor center*, not *the park visitor center's museum*.

quotation marks

Do not set off nicknames of trees or mountains in quotation marks. *Baldy*, not "*Baldy*."

sans serif font

Use a sans serif font for the single letter in *U-shaped* or *V-shaped*. Use regular font for other terms with single letters, such as *T-shirt, U-turn, J stroke*.

semicolon

Semicolons are used between the two parts of a compound sentence: *The left fork of the trail leads to the lake; the right fork takes you back to the trailhead.* As in this example, a semicolon is best used when the two parts of the sentence are parallel in construction.

If in doubt about whether the semicolon is being used correctly, ask yourself: Could the semicolon be replaced with a period? If the answer is no, the semicolon is not correct. Wrong: *The left fork of the trail leads to the lake; the right fork back to the trailhead.*

that, who, which

That and *which* are not interchangeable. Use *that* to introduce a defining (or restrictive) clause. *The pack that is on the picnic table is mine.* The word clause beginning with *that* tells which pack is being discussed.

Use *which* to add information: *My pack, which was on the table, attracted a number of ants.*

Use *who* (and *whom*) for people and for animals with names.

Use *that* and *which* for inanimate objects and for animals without names.

Use discretion in editing quoted, informal speech.

who, whom

Use *who* for the subject of a clause: *Who's there? The man who went hiking forgot his backpack.*

Use *whom* for an object of a verb or preposition: *To whom does this land belong?*

Use discretion in editing quoted speech.

Usage

A partial list of words often confused or causing other usage problems (see entries in the A-to-Z portion of the book):

acclimate/acclimatize

adapt/adopt

affect/effect

allusion/illusion

among/between

ante-/anti-

any more/anymore

auger/augur

a while/awhile

bridal/bridle

capital/capitol

climactic/climatic

continuous/continual

ecology/environment

emigrant/immigrant

enormity/enormous

farther/further

fewer/less

hoard/horde

holistic, not *wholistic*

mantel/mantle

more than/over

pica/pika

principal/principle

renown/renowned

slough/slew

tufa/tuff

use/utilize

Also note the following word pairs, unfortunate and common typos that spell check programs miss.

hoarse/horse

dairy/diary

trail/trial

Maps, Roads, and Directions

Road names

Numbered roads and highways: Give full names in the forms *Interstate 90, U.S. Highway 89, Montana Highway 200, County Road 434, BLM Road 75, Forest Road 2023.* If road names are mentioned occasionally, use the full name at each mention. In a text with many road names (such as a scenic driving guide), use the full name for major roads on first reference and the short form on second reference: *I-90, US 89, MT 200, County 434 (or CR 434), BLM 75, FR 2023.* When a short form would begin a sentence, either recast the sentence or write out the full name.

Do not use generic names like *route* or *state highway* to identify a road.

Named roads and city streets: Road name usage varies from

state to state. Sometimes numbered highways and interstates are referred to locally by names (for example, in one city *U.S. Highway 61* might be more commonly referred to as *Veterans Memorial Highway*). Follow local usage, but be sure that directions are comprehensible to someone who is not from the area. For clarity, if the road is known more commonly by the name of a town than by a number, do not use *the* before the name: Take *Carmel Valley Road*, not *the Carmel Valley Road* or *the Carmel Valley road*.

Capitalize special appellations for roads, and do not set off by quotation marks: *Avenue of the Giants, the Extraterrestrial Highway*.

Some road names may seem so generic as to raise doubts about their status as proper names: in a park, is it *a loop drive* or *the Loop Drive?* We recommend following park usage when stating full names of such roads: *the Scenic Drive* at Capitol Reef National Park. But if the full name consists of more than a generic term, as in *the Zion Canyon Scenic Drive*, then write *the scenic drive* on second reference.

Note the hyphens in such names as *Farm-to-Market Road*.

For numbered roads (not highways or interstates), spell out numbers from one to ten: *Fifth Avenue, 42nd Street*. Use numerals when the number follows the term: *Road 8, Road 27A* (also *Trail 6, exit 39, mile marker 22*).

Spell out directional terms that are part of a street name: *North Reserve Street*. Abbreviations such as *NW, NE, SE*, and *SW* are acceptable in guidebooks.

Use numerals for the actual street address: *555 Fuller Avenue*.

The preceding rules apply to road names in running text. In columns of addresses, as in an appendix, it is acceptable to abbreviate addresses in the form:

> Falcon Publishing
> P.O. Box 1718
> Helena, MT 59624

The abbreviation *P.O. Box* is always acceptable.

directions

Spell out compass directions in text and directional terms that are part of addresses. See individual entries under *west, east, north,* and *south* for information on capitalization of directional terms.

When describing mileage directions, "*at* x miles" should be reserved for mileage counts made from the starting point, and "*in* x miles" for incremental mileages between points mentioned in the directions. Thus, "From the Clark Fork Bridge in Missoula, head east. At 5.5 miles, turn left onto Holofernes Road. In another 2 miles, turn right onto Reserve Boulevard." For more on mileages, see **mile**.

meridian

Lowercase when stating longitude, and use numerals: *the 180th meridian.*

parallel

Lowercase when stating latitude, and use numerals: *the 40th parallel.*

Names and Capitalization

Individual names, geographical and administrative terms that often appear as part of a name, and phrases appear in the A-to-Z section of this book. What follows here is a summary of rules and guidelines for capitalization that we have found most useful in working with outdoor writing.

administrative designations

Capitalize a term like *national park* when it is part of the name of a place: *Yellowstone National Park.* Lowercase when used alone: *Yellowstone is a national park.*

Capitalization of administrative designations that are not

part of a place name may sometimes be desirable to avoid ambiguity and highlight the term as a designation. Terms that fall into this category include *national historic landmark* and *national natural landmark*. When such terms are capitalized, each word of the formal designation should be capitalized: *National Natural Landmark*, never *national Natural Landmark*.

For clarity, capitalize designations given to places by groups other than U.S. state and federal agencies: *Biosphere Reserve, National Champion Tree*. Such terms are thus handled similarly to **awards**. If necessary, add a few words of explanation about the significance of the designation.

brand names

Capitalize registered trademarks, as well as brand names, which are not necessarily registered but which signify a distinctive product associated with one manufacturer. The symbols ® and ™ need not appear in text following a capitalized trade name: "A *Gore-Tex* jacket is a must in this rainy climate." (Symbols may appear on book jackets, with no space between the word and the symbol.) Trademarks often appear in all capitals in advertising, but in ordinary text they may be capitalized as any other word: FalconGuide®.

Note: There is a tendency, over time, for certain brand names to pass into generic usage *(loafer, windbreaker, thermos)*. In rock climbing usage, the tendency is often accelerated, so that *jumaring* is commonly used as a verb (from *Jumar*, the name of a kind of ascender) and brand names such as *Stoppers* and *Hexes* are often seen in lowercase form. Although it is always preferable to capitalize brand names and choose generic terms if you wish to avoid a page that is sprinkled with capital letters, consistency is most important.

Always capitalize brands of fishing lures and types of fly patterns.

buildings

If a building is a landmark or otherwise considered a destination for visitors, and *building* is commonly considered part of the name, then capitalize the word: *Empire State Building*.

Lowercase when merely a descriptive term. Note that the term *capitol building* is redundant; a capitol is a building.

In general, capitalize the names of institutional buildings such as churches, libraries, museums, and schools. Also capitalize the names of buildings that are historic sites and/or destinations for visitors and managed as such: *Scotty's Castle, the Palace of the Governors, the Robert Louis Stevenson House.*

common names of plants and animals

Common names are not capitalized except for words that are proper nouns: *gray wolf, mule deer, western meadowlark, Townsend's pocket gopher, Swainson's hawk, Canada goose.* Note: this rule applies to general text. In Falcon wildflower, wildlife, and birding guides, Audubon field guide usage (in which all animal and plant names are fully capitalized) applies.

conforming with another group's usage

Often, terms that are ordinarily lowercase when used alone—*park, museum*—are capitalized in publications and advertising materials produced by that particular park or museum. This style need not be followed except in the case of cooperative publishing projects, when the agency should be consulted to ensure that the project meets the agency's style requirements.

events

Incidents, whether acts of nature or of human beings, are not usually capitalized except for words that are proper nouns: *the Loma Prieta earthquake, the Exxon Valdez oil spill.* This is the case even for historically significant incidents: *the San Francisco earthquake of 1906.* Exception: names of hurricanes are capitalized (*Hurricane Andrew*).

first and subsequent references

On first reference, always give the full names of places, organizations, and so on. This is particularly important in guidebooks, which are often not read through from beginning to end. If the *Appalachian Trail* is mentioned in chapter 1 and subsequently abbreviated as *AT*, on the first reference in chapter 2, it should again be referred to as the *Appalachian Trail*.

Likewise, do not use a short form of a name in a caption unless the full name has already appeared in a caption within that chapter.

geographical terms

In general, terms that commonly appear in the names of places are capitalized. Such terms include, but are not limited to, lakes, rivers, waterfalls, and beaches; mountains, cliffs, points, rocks, and landforms; plateaus, mesas, and valleys.

Some of these same terms may function as descriptive terms when they follow an already complete geographic name: *the Goosenecks Overlook*, but *the Inspiration Point overlook*.

More problematic are terms such as *delta* and *valley*. In practice, when a complete geographical name is followed by one of these terms, the entire name is commonly capitalized when it represents the name of a large, populated region: *Mississippi River Delta*. When the area in question is small or not significantly inhabited by people, *delta* or *valley* may be taken as a descriptive term: *Nisqually River delta*. Terms such as *delta*, *valley*, and *coast* are also considered descriptive when the context refers to a physical location, not a populated place: *tidepools of the Pacific coast*, but *beach towns of the West Coast*.

geological terms

Terms that refer to formations and eras are considered descriptive, and need not be capitalized. Thus: *Cutler formation*, *Morrison formation*, *Entrada sandstone*, *Mancos shale*, *Paleozoic era*.

groups

Apostrophes often do not appear in group names that look as if they are possessives: *Idaho Outfitters and Guides Association*. In this example, "Outfitters and Guides" is attributive, modifying "Association." A similar construction is seen in the term *citizens band*, which also has no apostrophe. Such names should be verified, however: *International Ladies' Garment Workers Union*.

historically significant terms

Capitalize appellations given to historically significant people and groups: *Big Four, Copper Kings, Donner Party, Hayden Survey.*

Major periods of human development, *the Stone Age, Bronze Age,* and *Iron Age,* are capitalized. Contemporary terms such as *atomic age* or *information age,* while often capitalized in newspapers and magazines, should be lowercase.

nicknames

Capitalize names such as *Bigfoot, the Jersey Devil, Kennewick Man.* Also capitalize nicknames given to trees and mountains, and do not set off by quotation marks: *General Sherman, Baldy.* Nicknames of trees and mountains should only be used on second reference.

place names

Authoritative sources for place names include the *National Five-Digit ZIP Code and Post Office Directory* for names of populated places and the geographic names database of the U.S. Geological Survey website, www.usgs.gov, for names of landforms. The Canadian government offers a database for Canadian place names, geonames.nrcan.gc.ca.

Background note: The U.S. Board on Geographic Names is the final arbiter of official forms of U.S. place names. The board's policy is to avoid accents and apostrophes. Thus: *Zuni, Devils Tower.* The board's policy is also to prefer one-word compounds for populated places and to avoid hyphens. This offers a rationale for such apparent inconsistencies as the following:

• *Ship Rock,* the rock formation in New Mexico, is two words, but the town of *Shiprock* is one.

• The word *twenty-nine* has a hyphen, but the town of *Twentynine Palms,* California, has none.

When local usage differs from the official form of the name, it may take precedence; such decisions should be made on a case-by-case basis.

migration routes: Major bird migration routes are considered proper names and capitalized *(Pacific Flyway, Mississippi Flyway)*.

numbers as part of names: When the name of a city or town includes a number, the number is usually spelled out: *Twentynine Palms, California; Three Forks, Montana; Ninemile, Montana; Fortymile River, Alaska.* Check the *National Five-Digit ZIP Code and Post Office Directory* for the correct form of the name of a populated place. Numbers in names of campgrounds, trails, and highway exits may appear as numerals.

regions: Capitalize terms that are commonly used as the name of a region: *the Texas Hill Country, the New Jersey Pine Barrens.* Follow regional usage, when appropriate. For example, capitalize *the San Francisco Bay Area* and the *Bay Area*, but do not capitalize *the City* when referring to San Francisco (although this is often done in Bay Area newspapers).

roads: *Avenue, street, highway,* and other terms for roads are capitalized when part of a formal name *(Laguna Street, Beartooth Highway),* but when these words stand alone, they are lowercase *(the street, the highway).* Exception: Spanish-language terms remain capitalized when used alone, if the term is not commonly used in English as a generic synonym for street *(Alameda de las Pulgas, the Alameda; Paseo de Peralta, the Paseo).*

For more on roads, see **Maps, Roads, and Directions,** pg. 14.

trail, trailhead: Capitalize *trail* when part of the formal name of a hiking trail or historic trail: *Pacific Crest Trail, Oregon Trail.* Capitalize *trailhead* only when part of a formal name (consult the land management agency if necessary): *Multnomah Falls Trailhead.* For numbered trails, do not use the # symbol or the abbreviation *No.* before the number: *Trail 62.* When several trails or trailheads are mentioned in a description of a hike, to avoid confusion, clearly state each trail name or number on each reference. When only one trail is being discussed, *the trail* is okay on second reference.

plurals

Capitalize terms such as *lake, river, mountains,* and so on, when used as apart of a place name, in singular and plural, before or after the name: *Flathead Lake, Lake Louise, Flathead and Hebgen Lakes.* This conforms with the *Chicago Manual of Style,* 14th ed. (a change in style from the 13th ed.). The same rule applies to road names: *Montana Highway 200, Montana Highways 200 and 135.*

scientific names

Scientific names are best dealt with on a case-by-case basis. Occasionally names are revised, as species are reclassified as subspecies or vice versa. Use the *American Heritage Dictionary* and current editions of Audubon field guides and taxonomic publications to determine the most appropriate spelling of the Latin name of a plant or animal.

The following general rules apply: In a name of the form *Canis lupus* (gray wolf), the first word is the genus name, the second is the species name. The genus name is capitalized; the species name is lowercase. Both are italicized.

Genus and species names can be the same: *Alces alces* (the moose). Subspecies names, when used, follow species names and also are italicized: *Alces alces shirasi.* In scientific names, the species name is always lowercase, even when derived from a person's name or from a former genus: *Lesquerella gordoni.* However, when a subspecies is distinguished by the discoverer's name, that name is not italicized: *Bufo woodhousei* Woodhouse.

On first reference, give the complete genus and species name. On second reference, the genus name can be abbreviated: *C. lupus.*

Additional designations such as *sp.* or *var.* are in roman type following the name. A lowercase *sp.* following a genus name indicates that the species is not specified: *Arbutus* sp. (a madrone of some kind). A lowercase *var.* following a genus and species name indicates a variety: *Arbutus menziesii* var.

Larger divisions than genus, such as class, order, and family, are capitalized and set in roman type: Mustelidae family (weasels and skunks). Note that *family* is lowercase. Lowercase and roman type for the English version of a Latin family name: mustelids.

seasons

Do not capitalize *spring, summer, fall/autumn,* or *winter,* except in bibliographic reference to periodicals: *Big Sky Journal,* Spring 1997.

Nondiscriminatory Language

Falcon is committed to a policy of nonsexist, nondiscriminatory language in every book it publishes. We expect a respectful attitude toward all ethnicities, traditions, and sexual orientations from everyone who works on a Falcon book. In addition, we encourage authors and editors to apply the local forms of proper names in regional books; this is particularly important regarding the names of Indians and Indian tribes.

The only exception to this policy is the presentation of offensive language in direct quotes or in books of a historical nature (usually first-person narratives) for the sake of accuracy.

WRITING WITHOUT GENDER BIAS

The Handbook of Nonsexist Writing, ed. Casey Miller and Kate Swift (New York: Harper & Row, 1988) is the classic treatment of gender bias in writing, with many good and often humorous examples.

Be aware of the following:

Jobs, Activities, Social roles

-man endings: In most cases there is a gender-neutral term that is not awkward (chairperson) and that also avoids the chairman/chairwoman endings. For example:

fly fisherman	fly fisher
horseman	rider
weatherman	weather forecaster, meteorologist

Miller and Swift suggest the U.S. Department of Labor's *Dictionary of Occupational Titles* as a source of gender-neutral titles, such as *fisher,* not *fisherman.*

Terms for practitioners of outdoor activities rarely take the kind of feminine ending *(-ess, -trix)* that should be avoided unless, for instance, you are writing about the huntress, the Greek goddess Diana. Instead, gender bias can appear in what Miller and Swift call "assigning gender to gender-neutral terms." A fly fisher may be either male or female, a phrase like "ranchers and their wives" assumes that all ranchers are male.

Be careful, also, of pointing out that a certain practitioner of an outdoor activity is a woman. Do not write *woman climber Lynn Hill* unless you are prepared to write *man climber John Long.* Similarly, if a woman is the first to do something that has only been done before by men, it would be appropriate to write something like *the first woman to climb Mount Everest.* If, however, a certain peak has never been climbed by anyone, then write *the first person to climb* or *the first climber to summit,* whether that person is a man or a woman.

Exception: In certain historical contexts, it is appropriate to reflect the gender bias of the period. Feel free to refer to *mountain men.* Also, terms now considered offensive, like *squaw,* appear often in original historical material. Some such names have been changed over time, and some local place names with *Squaw* are being changed now. An editor's note may be appropriate to indicate that the publisher is aware that some terms are now considered offensive.

first and last names: Be consistent when referring to people. Do not refer to Lynn Hill as Lynn, but John Long as Long.

inanimate objects: Ships, countries, and other inanimate objects should always be referred to as *it.* Use discretion in editing quoted speech, however, as the speaker's assumptions may be an important part of the meaning.

man, mankind: It is now common practice to avoid the use of *man* or *mankind* to refer to all human beings. Instead of *the men who have helped preserve America's wilderness,* write *people who have* *helped preserve America's wilderness.* In describing an archaeological site, instead of referring to *ancient man, early man,* or *Cro-Magnon man,* write *ancient people, inhabitants,* or *residents, Cro-Magnon people,* and so on. Obviously, in a case where a specific person is being discussed, it is not inappropriate to assign gender: a female mummy is a she, Kennewick Man is a he.

manmade: Some people object to this term. Alternatives are available: *made by hand, artificially constructed, manufactured.*

order in which people are listed: It is easy to fall into the pattern of giving first a male, then a female example. I did it myself, in my first draft, when what originally appeared a few lines before was *Kennewick man is a he, a female mummy a she.*

outdoorsman, outdoorswoman: Although the word *outdoorsman,* when used alone, may give the impression of excluding women, the word *outdoorswoman* is used by some groups to make the point that women are also participants in traditional outdoor activities such as hunting and fishing. An example is the name of the program *Becoming an Outdoors-Woman* (the hyphen is theirs). For a term that is not gender-specific, try *outdoors enthusiasts* or *people who enjoy the outdoors.*

phenomena: Hurricanes are given male and female names, but Hurricane Andrew is an *it.* So is Hurricane Betty. There is no need for Hurricane Betty to flirt with a coastline, or for Hurricane Andrew to marshal his forces. (The same goes for attributing human gender stereotypes to animals.) In general, aspects of nature should not be personified. Nature is an *it,* not a *she.*

Exception: If the context is an American Indian story, animals and forces of nature may be personified: *"Coyote knew he was in big trouble."*

pronouns: Many terms for participants in outdoor activities do not, in themselves, indicate whether the person is male or female: *climber, hunter, park ranger.* Problems arise in handling pronouns and singulars and plurals. A term like *he or she* is unwieldy when it appears more than a few times in a text.

To solve problems, some writers like to alternate the terms:

she in one section, *he* in another. If this is your choice, be aware of the context in which each pronoun appears. In a book about climbing techniques, it might be insensitive to refer to Climber X as *he*, until the section on rescues, at which point Climber X is a she who is in need of rescue.

Since changes from *he* to *she* can be distracting to the reader, a better solution is to recast sentences in the plural. Instead of *a climber should check his knot*, or *a climber should check his or her knot*, write *climbers should check their knots*.

Never use *they* or *their* when your subject is singular. Wrong: *A backcountry hiker should leave only their footprints.* Right: *Backcountry hikers should leave only their footprints.*

Another alternative is to use the second person: *You should leave only footprints.* Sometimes you can even leave out the pronoun: *Backcountry hikers should leave only footprints.*

writers' assumptions about readers: Gender bias can affect writers' assumptions about readers as well as treatment of subjects. "The T-shirt and boxer shorts you wore in summer and fall should be the first clothes you put on," says one recently published traditional "outdoorsman's" guide in a section on cold-weather clothing.

animals

Use *it* to refer to an animal that has no personal name, whether the context is personal experience or field guide description: "I spotted the bear right away. It was huge." If writing about porcupines: "Coyotes and bobcats are *its* natural enemies," not "*his* natural enemies." Do not assume that an animal is male or female.

When the context makes it clear that the animal must be male or female, it is acceptable to refer to the animal as *he* or *she:* The mother grizzly bear kept an eye on *her* cubs. In a field guide, such distinctions should be easy to make. In a narrative, inconsistencies can arise, with animals being referred to as *it* and *he* or *she* within the same paragraph or two. In such cases, it is preferable to establish the sex of the animal early on and use the appropriate pronoun consistently. Alternatively, you can stick with *it*.

There can be no objection to using gendered pronouns to refer to animals who have names (or referring to them as *who* instead of *that*). "My dog, Bob, ran up with a happy grin on *his* face." The same rule would apply to wild animals, even when their sex is irrelevant to the context, such as when a few animals are frequently observed in a location and have been given names by the observers.

WRITING WITHOUT RACIAL BIAS

Racial bias in writing is much less common today, but as with gender bias, it may be present in original historical material. An editor's note may be appropriate to indicate awareness of such material.

If you are issuing a reprint of an older title, be aware that the book may contain out-of-date terms for place names and even common names of plants *(niggerhead cactus)* that are now considered racially offensive. Most such place names have been changed *(Negro Bill Canyon*, near Moab, Utah). In a new edition, such terms can be corrected silently.

Background note: The U.S. Board on Geographic Names is the federal agency that establishes official place names in the United States. (States also have geographic names boards.) In the 1960s, the U.S. Board on Geographic Names changed all U.S. place names that included the word *Nigger* to *Negro*. Place names that include the term *Squaw* are undergoing similar review today, often at the local or state level before going to the federal board for a final decision.

Numbers

For guidebooks and field guides, which usually contain many numbers, we recommend the following:

Measurements: Use numerals for all measurements, even

those under ten, for distance, temperature, weight, caliber, angles (degrees). Units of time and age are not considered measurements; thus, write out *a one-hour drive, a three-day trip, a four-year-old child.*

Enumeration: For numbers that represent enumeration, not measurement, write out from one to ten. Use numerals over ten.

Tables, charts, maps: Use numerals.

Large numbers: For numbers of 1 million and larger, use the form *4.5 billion years; 65 million years ago.* Applies to money also: *$3 million.* (Not *$3 million dollars.*)

Consistency: When numbers represent enumeration, if one number in a sentence must be written as a numeral, write all numbers in that sentence as numerals: *I saw 17 prairie dogs and 2 rattlesnakes that day.* If such numbers appear throughout a passage of a paragraph or more, treat them consistently. The goal is to avoid distracting the reader by switching between spelled-out numbers and numerals. Note: Measurements and spelled-out numbers representing enumeration may appear in the same sentence without inconsistency. *Go 2 miles down the trail until you come to a clearing with three large boulders.*

These rules are intended to promote easy access to the factual information contained in guidebooks and field guides. For outdoor-related writing that does not contain many numbers, the *Chicago Manual of Style* rules still apply.

The following examples illustrate forms of numbers and treatment of numbers in particular topics:

caliber

No hyphen when measured in millimeters: *a 9 mm pistol.*

Use a hyphen when measured in decimal fractions of an inch: *a .22-caliber rifle, a .45-caliber revolver.*

climbing

In climbing guidebooks, use numerals when referring to

number of pitches and sizes of gear. The symbol ' for *foot* is acceptable, too. *A 3-pitch climb; a 130' cliff.*

comma

Use a comma to indicate the thousands place: *a 5,500-foot peak.*

dates

Write dates in month-day-year order. In running text, the year should be set off by commas: She was born on *August 10, 1955,* in New York. No comma is used when the date consists of a month and year only: *August 1955.*

Years: *1960,* not *'60.* Decades: *1960s,* not *1960's* or *the sixties.* Spell out terms like *Roaring Twenties.* Centuries are always spelled out: *the end of the twentieth century; a twentieth-century invention.* Link a range of years with an en dash, and always give the full year: *1960–1970,* not *1960–70.*

Avoid beginning a sentence with a year, because it must then be spelled out. Instead of *"Nineteen eighty-nine* was a year of drought," rewrite as "There was a drought in *1989."*

degrees

Use numerals for measurements: *a 360-degree view, a 45-degree slope, a slope of 45 degrees.* Spell out the number when referring to burns: *first-degree burn.*

distances

Use decimals to indicate fractions of a mile: *1.5 miles, 10.7 miles.* For whole numbers, do not use a decimal unless emphasizing the accuracy of the mileage point: *"At 2.0 mile,* turn left onto Forest Road 2023;" but *"After 2 miles,* the trail begins to climb."

For distances of less than 1 mile, use the singular: *0.5 mile,* not *0.5 miles.* Always use a zero before the decimal.

When approximating distances of less than a mile, write out *a quarter of a mile, a third of a mile, half a mile,* preceded by the word *about,* instead of *about 0.5 mile* or *about 0.33 mile.* The same principle applies to approximations of **time.**

figures of speech

Spell out expressions like *number one, half-baked,* or *his thoughts were a thousand miles away.*

fishing

Use numerals when stating the weight of a line, length and weight of a rod, or size of a hook: *a 4-weight fly line, an 8-foot rod, a 6-weight rod, a No. 4 hook.* Do not use the # symbol for any of these sizes.

fractions

In measurements, express fractions as decimals: *8.75 miles, 3.5 feet.* If the fraction is less than 1, use a zero before the decimal point: *0.5 mile, 0.75 foot.* Note that the unit of measurement is then singular, not plural.

In figures of speech, spell out fractions: *"Gorging yourself on huckleberries is half the fun."* Also spell out approximate times and measurements: *The sun rose around half past six.*

hyphenation

Hyphenate compound modifiers before a noun: *a 200-pound bear.* No hyphen after the noun: *the bear weighed 200 pounds.* Applies to measurements of height, weight, length. Also applies to ages and units of time.

metric system

Metric measurements are used for measurement of caliber, sizes of film, and sizes of rope or cord. For millimeters, use the abbreviation mm: *a 9 mm pistol, 35 mm film, 6 mm cord.* For clarity, spell out a number of enumeration that immediately precedes a measurement: *Take two 10 mm ropes.*

Metric abbreviations are not followed by a period, unless they fall at the end of a sentence.

Do not use metric terms for weights or distances except in a book intended for a Canadian or other non-American audience, or to conform to a land management agency's usage. If metric measurements are called for, do not abbreviate the meters or kilograms: *50 meters, 500 kilograms, 9 kilometers,* not *50 m,*

500 kg, 9 km. When including both English and metric measurements, separate measurements with a slash, flanked by single spaces: *3.5 in. / 8.8 cm.* Dimensions: *3.5 in. x 6 in. / 8.8 cm x 15.24 cm.*

Two instances in which metric measurements are commonly used in an American context: *2-liter bottles* and *10-kilometer races.*

money

If you can write the amount and the word *dollars* in two words, write it out: *five dollars, fifty dollars.* Exception: in guidebooks, use only numerals (*$5, $50*).

If the amount plus the word *dollars* is three or more words, use numerals and the dollar sign: *$55, $100* (not *$100.00*), *$5.75.*

The same rules apply to amounts in cents (use the dollar sign, not the cents sign): *fifty cents,* but *$.98,* not *98¢* or *ninety-eight cents.*

The same rules apply to forms of currency of other countries.

names of products and businesses

Follow their preference: *7-Eleven, Motel 6.*

percentage

Use numerals: *50 percent, 99 percent.* Not *per cent* or *%.*

place names

When the name of a city or town includes a number, the number is usually spelled out: *Twentynine Palms, California; Three Forks, Montana; Ninemile, Montana; Fortymile River, Alaska.* Check the *National Five-Digit ZIP Code and Post Office Directory* for the correct form of the name of a populated place. Hyphens do not usually appear in place names, even when they would appear in the ordinary form of the word.

Numbers in names of campgrounds, trails, and highway exits appear as numerals: *Trail 6, exit 14, mile marker 22.*

roads

See **Maps, Roads, and Directions,** p. 14.

temperature

In text, use the abbreviation *F* (no period) instead of the word *Fahrenheit: 57 degrees F.* To give a range of temperatures: *The temperature can drop 15 to 20 degrees after sundown.* To give negative temperatures: *-15 degrees F* or *15 below zero,* not *minus 15.* Spell out the word *zero.* In January, *below-zero* temperatures are not unusual.

In cookbooks and hot springs guides, use the degree symbol: *Bake at 375° for 3 hours.* Fahrenheit temperatures are assumed.

time of day

Small caps, with no space between the elements: *6 A.M. (not 6:00 A.M.), 5:30 P.M., open from 1 to 4:30 P.M.*

If referring generally to a half-hour or quarter-hour, spell out: We arrived *around half past four,* not *around 4:30.* Use numerals if the precise time is important, as in giving hours of operation. The same principle applies to approximations of **distance.**

units of measure

Spell out the terms *miles, feet, yards,* and other units of measurement, except in rock climbing guides and field guides. Field guides use the abbreviations *ft., in., cm, mm.* Wildflower field guides use the symbols *'* and *"* for *feet* and *inches.* Rock climbing guides use the symbol *'* for *feet.*

Use the abbreviation *mm* for caliber of guns and sizes of film, rope, and cord.

Metric abbreviations are not followed by a period, unless they fall at the end of a sentence.

When including both English and metric measurements, separate measurements with a slash, flanked by single spaces: *3.5 in. / 8.8 cm.* Dimensions: *3.5 in. 6 in. / 8.8 cm x 15.24 cm.*

Temperature

Celsius

Not *centigrade.* In text, use the abbreviation *C* (no period): *20 degrees C.* But use **Fahrenheit** temperatures in books for U.S. audiences.

Fahrenheit

In text, use the abbreviation *F* (no period) instead of the word *Fahrenheit: 57 degrees F.* To give a range of temperatures: *The temperature can drop 15 to 20 degrees after sundown.* To give a general idea of the temperature: *summertime highs in the 90s.*

To give negative temperatures: *-15 degrees F* or *15 below zero,* not *minus 15.*

In cookbooks and hot springs guides, use the degree symbol: *Bake at 375° for 3 hours.* Fahrenheit temperatures are assumed.

zero

Spell out the word *zero,* as in *15 below zero.* "In January, *below-zero* temperatures are not unusual." "For one week in December, the temperature never rose above *zero.*"

Weather

directions

Lowercase directional terms when referring to weather: *a west wind, a storm from the north.* Capitalize *Arctic* when referring specifically to a storm that is coming from the Arctic. Lowercase *arctic* when the meaning is simply "very cold."

events

Names of hurricanes are capitalized and set in roman type: *Hurricane Andrew.*

Other events, such as notable storms, are normally lowercased: *the blizzard of 1989* (even though such events may be capitalized in newspaper reports).

National Weather Service

On second reference, *the weather service* (lowercase). No longer called the *U.S. Weather Bureau* or *the weather bureau.*

phenomena

Terms for clouds, winds, and other weather phenomena are not capitalized, except for words that are proper nouns. Thus, *aurora borealis, northern lights, chinook, cirrus* are all lowercase; but capitalize the wind called *Santa Ana.*

Some weather phenomena have been given names: *El Niño, La Niña.*

Outdoor Style
from A to Z

A

a- Adverbs formed with the prefix *a-* are written as one word, never with a hyphen: *afoot, astride.* But *horseback* or *on horseback,* rather than *ahorseback,* except informally (as in quoted speech).

Abbey, Edward (1927–1989) author of *Desert Solitaire* and *The Monkey Wrench Gang.*

abbreviations See **Abbreviations and Acronyms,** p. 4.

about/approximately *about* preferred as shorter and less formal.

above/below Do not use to refer to material mentioned earlier in the text; instead, use preceding/following or earlier/later.

Absaroka Range, the Absarokas

abseil synonym for **rappel;** typically a British usage. Use **rappel** instead.

academic degrees Capitalize, with periods when abbreviated: *B.A., M.D., M.F.A., Ph.D.* No spaces between the elements.

When spelled out and referred to generally, academic degrees are lowercase: a *master's degree* in forestry.

academic fields, departments, classes Lowercase unless a proper name: She has a degree in *environmental studies.* He teaches *literature of natural history* in the *English department.*

accents In general, use accents if they are part of the accepted spelling of place names in the United States.

A regional spelling with accents—as with Spanish place names in California and the Southwest—may sometimes take precedence over the commonly accepted spelling. For Canadian place names, use the English spelling *(Quebec, Montreal)*, not the French *(Québec, Montréal)*.

Names of Indian tribes: *Nez Perce, Zuni, Diegueño, Luiseño.*

See individual entries for forms of specific words, such as *arête, névé, El Niño.*

accidental describes a bird out of its normal range.

Accidents in North American Mountaineering annual publication of American Alpine Club and Alpine Club of Canada.

acclimate/acclimatize *Acclimate* means to adapt, generally; *acclimatize* means more specifically adapting to conditions such as climate or elevation.

Ace bandage

ACEC See **area of critical environmental concern.**

acequia Spanish for an irrigation ditch; term used in the Southwest. Not italicized.

acknowledgments not *acknowledgements.*

Aconcagua mountain in Argentina; highest peak in Western Hemisphere (22,834 feet).

acre-foot, acre-feet the volume of water that would cover an area of one acre one foot deep.

acronyms See **Abbreviations and Acronyms,** p. 4.

act Capitalize when part of the name of an act: *the Endangered Species Act,* but *the act.*

A.D. abbreviation for *anno domini,* "in the year of our Lord." Small caps, with periods, and no space between the elements. Always precedes the year: Chinese astronomers observed the supernova in A.D. *1054.* Also see B.C., B.C.E., C.E.

adapt/adopt *Adapt* means to modify or change: *adapt* to new conditions. One *adopts* a child.

addresses See **Maps, Roads, and Directions,** p. 14.

Adirondack Mountain Club The club's magazine is called *Adirondac.*

Adirondack Park a New York state park, not a national park.

adrenaline *Adrenalin* is a trademark.

aero- The root means "air": *aerodynamic, aerobic, anaerobic.*

affect/effect *Affect* as a verb means to produce an effect on: The storm *affected* their camping plans. As a verb, *effect* is to bring about: The legislation should *effect* an improvement in water quality.

A-frame (n.)

African American (n.), **African-American** (adj.), or **Black** (n., adj.)

afterward not *afterwards.*

afterword an epilogue.

Agassiz, Louis (1807–1873) naturalist and geologist.

age Capitalize *Stone Age, Iron Age,* and *Bronze Age.* Lowercase **ice age** and names for modern times such as *atomic age.* Also see **centuries, decades, eras.**

ages of people, places Spell out ages of people: She is *thirty years old.* Hyphenate an age when it appears before a noun: They took their *two-year-old* daughter on a rafting trip. Also hyphenate when the age stands alone as a noun: a group of *ten-year-olds.*

Ahwahnee Hotel a lodge at Yosemite National Park.

aid climbing style of rock climbing that involves placing weight directly on ropes and other gear.

Grades I to VI rate the time needed to complete the route. The decimal rating rates the difficulty of the climb. Grades A1 to A5 rate the placements of aid gear. If the letter A is replaced by the letter C (for example, C2 rather than A2), then the rating applies to the route when it is climbed clean, with chocks, not pitons.

Form of rating for aid climbing route: VI, 5.10, A2.

aiders also called **etriers.**

aiguille mountain peak that comes to a point; a French
word, but do not italicize.

air Compound nouns with *air* are usually written as two
words: *air bag, air bladder, air cushion, air sac, air taxi,* but *airway.*

air conditioning (n.), **air-condition** (v.), **air-conditioned**
(adj.)

airfield, air base

air force See **armed forces.**

airline(s) *Airline* is one word generally, but appears as two
words in the names of some airlines.

airport Capitalize when part of the full formal name: *Salt
Lake City International Airport, the Salt Lake City airport.* Names
should be checked, as the name of a city or town com-
bined with *airport* does not necessarily yield the proper
name. *Durango–La Plata County Airport,* not the *Durango
Airport* (note the en dash connecting a two-word name
with another word).

Airstream trailer.

Alaska Highway not *Alcan Highway,* the former name.

Alaska Marine Highway System or *the Alaska state ferry.*

Alaska Native *an Alaska Native village, an Alaska Native corporation.*

Alaska Railroad

Alaska standard time

Albright, Horace M. (1890–1987) cofounder of the
National Park Service.

alderfly

Aleutian

alfresco One word. No need to italicize.

Alien Capitalize for the brand name of a camming device.

Allegheny Mountains, the Alleghenies but *Allegany* Counties
in Maryland and New York; *Alleghany* Counties in North
Carolina and Virginia. Also *Allegheny, Alleghenian* in geolog-

ical terms referring to the mountain-building event.

all right (adv., adj.) never *alright* or *all-right*.

allude/elude To *allude* is to refer indirectly; to *elude* is to evade or escape.

alluvial fan

alpenglow

alpine Lowercase, *alpine* refers generally to high mountains. Capitalized, it refers specifically to the Alps.

alpine skiing refers to any kind of skiing in which a rigid binding locks the heel to the ski, as in traditional **downhill skiing**.

altitude height above sea level, or, generally, a high area; often a synonym for **elevation**.

altitude sickness also called **mountain sickness**.

A.M. Small caps, with no space between the elements: *6 A.M.* (not *6:00 A.M.*), *5:30 P.M., open from 1 to 4:30 P.M.* (Note: There are no periods in *AM radio*, and full-size letters are used.)

America *North America, Central America, South America.* Likewise, capitalize the adjective forms. Also see **United States** for regions.

American Compound nouns are not hyphenated: *African American, Chinese American.* Hyphenate the adjective forms: *African-American.* Note: *Native American* (n., adj.) has no hyphen. Also see **ethnicity**.

American Alpine Club but *Alpine Club of Canada.*

American Automobile Association, AAA

American Fur Company established by John Jacob Astor.

American Indian preferred over *Native American.* See **Indian** and **Appendix B: Indian tribes.**

American Red Cross

American Revolution also *the Revolutionary War, the Revolution.*

Amon Carter Museum of Western Art in Fort Worth, Texas.

among See usage note at **between/among.**

ampersand/and If used consistently, ampersands are acceptable in names of railroads and other corporate names: *Smith & Wesson.* Ampersands are also acceptable in names of government agencies, if that is the agency's preferred style: *Montana Department of Fish, Wildlife & Parks.* In a bibliography, ampersands may be used in place of *and* in names of publishers (again, this should be consistent). When citing titles, an ampersand should be spelled out as *and.*

Amtrak not *AMTRAK.*

Amundsen, Roald (1872–1928) Norwegian explorer of the North and South Poles.

anadromous (adj.) refers to fish, such as salmon, that live in the ocean and spawn in freshwater.

Anasazi A prehistoric Indian culture of the Southwest. Because the term *Anasazi* is derived from the Navajo language, *Ancestral Pueblo* or *Ancestral Puebloan* are sometimes preferred. The term *cliff dweller* is out of date and should not be used except in historical references, but *Anasazi* is still acceptable.

Ancestral Pueblo(an) sometimes used in preference to **Anasazi.**

anchor Compound nouns with *anchor* include *artificial anchor* or *gear anchor, fixed anchor, natural anchor.*

angle piton also called an *angle.*

angler not *fisherman* or *fisherwoman.*

Anglo, Anglo-American (n., adj.) equivalent to **White,** usually in a Southwestern context.

Animal Damage Control (ADC) former name of a government program, now called **Wildlife Services,** part of the Animal and Plant Health Inspection Service, U.S. Department of Agriculture.

animal names Common names are lowercase except for words that are proper nouns: *gray wolf, California mouse.* Also see **taxonomy.**

animals, pronouns with Animals should be referred to as *it*, except when they have their own names, as is the case with a pet dog or horse. The bear raised *its* head. Animals may also be referred to as *he* or *she* when described in terms of a relationship that demands a gendered pronoun: Never get between a mother bear and *her* cubs. For an additional discussion, see **Nondiscriminatory language,** p. 23.

ankle-deep (adj.)

Antarctica the continent; *the Antarctic* is the region; *Antarctic* (adj.) Unlike *arctic, Antarctic* is always capitalized.

ante-/anti- The prefix *ante-* means "before," *anti-* means "against," "opposing," or "counteracting." Compounds with either prefix are generally written as one word: *antedate, anticline.*

antebellum refers to the period before the Civil War.

antelope *pronghorn antelope* or **pronghorn** preferred.

Antiquities Protection Act of 1906

antivenin not *antivenom.*

antlers are periodically shed and regrown (horns are permanent).

any more/anymore *Anymore* is an adverb referring to time: I used to ride without a helmet, but I don't *anymore. Any more* (two words) refers to quantity: Are there *any more* pancakes?

apatite a kind of mineral; not *appetite.*

Appalachia the region including the Appalachian Mountains.

Appalachian Trail runs from Springer Mountain, Georgia, to Mount Katahdin, Maine. **AT** acceptable on second reference.

appendix, appendixes preferred as plural over *appendices.*

approach in climbing, what precedes the actual start of a route.

aqua- This prefix means "water," as in *aquarium* and *aquatic,* but note the spellings of *aqueduct* and *aquifer.*

Aqua-Lung a trademark.

aqueduct

aquifer

Aransas a county in Texas; also *Port Aransas, Aransas Pass* (not *Arkansas*).

arboreal (adj.) relating to trees; not **boreal,** "northern."

arch Capitalize the name of an arch: *Delicate Arch,* but *the arch.*

Archaeological Resources Protection Act of 1979

archaeologist, archaeology preferred over *archeologist, archeology.*

Archaic Lowercase when the meaning is "primitive" or "of an early time" in a general sense, but capitalize when referring to the cultural era in the desert Southwest that preceded the more settled, agricultural societies of the Anasazi, Fremont, Hohokam, and Mogollon: *a cave used by Archaic hunter-gatherers.*

architectural styles Lowercase, except for words that are proper names: *art deco, arts and crafts, colonial* (the style in general), *Colonial* (a home that actually dates from the Colonial period).

arctic When capitalized, *Arctic* refers specifically to the region, as in the *Arctic Circle.* Lowercase generally, as in an *arctic wind,* and in names of species: *arctic fox.*

Arctic Cat a brand of snowmobile.

area Capitalize when part of a proper name: *Golden Gate National Recreation Area,* but *the national recreation area, the area.*

area of critical environmental concern a Bureau of Land Management designation. Capitalize only when necessary to avoid ambiguity or highlight the term's status as an official designation. Government agencies use the abbreviation *ACEC.*

arête

Arlington National Cemetery

armbar (n.) the rock climbing technique.

armed forces Capitalize *army* when referring to *U.S. Army,* the *Army;* also the *U.S. Navy* and *Air Force.* Lowercase when referring to other nations' armies (because the English translation may not reflect word-for-word the name of the military unit in the original language): the *Mexican army.*

arrowhead

arroyo, arroyos a deep, stream-cut gully where water runs intermittently.

artifact preferred over *artefact.*

artwork Proper names of paintings, sculpture, and other forms of artwork are italicized: Church's painting *The Heart of the Andes.* Charlie Russell's *Bronc to Breakfast.* Ansel Adams's photograph *Moonrise Over Hernandez.*

If the common name of a work of art is not the formal name of the piece, capitalize and set that name in roman type: *La Gioconda* is better known as the Mona Lisa.

as, such as, like *Like* is a preposition, which takes an object: He runs *like* a gazelle. *As* is a conjunction: He runs *as* a gazelle does. *Like* and *such as* are interchangeable when giving an example: *wildflowers such as arnica* or *wildflowers like arnica.*

ash juniper not *ashe juniper.*

AT acceptable second reference for the **Appalachian Trail.**

ATB an all-terrain bicycle, or mountain bike.

ATC acceptable second reference for *Air Traffic Controller,* a belay device made by Black Diamond.

Atlantic coast Lowercase when referring to the coastline: *beaches along the Atlantic coast.* When referring to the region, *the East Coast* is more common. Capitalize *North Atlantic, Mid-Atlantic states.*

atlatl

ATM automated/automatic teller machine; *ATM* okay on first reference.

atomic age

ATV, all-terrain vehicle

Audubon acceptable second reference for *National Audubon Society.*

Audubon, John James (1785–1851) American painter of birds and other wildlife.

auger/augur Use an *auger* (n.) to drill into ice when ice fishing. To *augur* (v.) is to predict or to be an omen of something: The sunny weather *augured* success for the expedition.

aurora borealis the northern lights. Lowercase, roman type. The corresponding phenomenon in the Southern Hemisphere is the *aurora australis*.

Austin, Mary (1868–1934) author of *The Land of Little Rain*.

avalanche (n.) slide of snow or rock down a mountainside (compare **landslide, mudslide, rockslide**).

avocet

awards Capitalize the full formal name of an award: *the Lee Wulff Conservation Award*, but *the Lee Wulff award, the Lee Wulff prize*. Also see **prizes, medals, Olympics**.

a while/awhile In the phrase *a while, while* is a noun and is always used with a preposition: We rested by the lake *for a while*. *Awhile* (one word) is an adverb and means "for a while." It is never used with a preposition: We rested *awhile* by the lake.

ax, axe Either is acceptable, but spelling should be consistent within a text. Don't write *ax* on one page and *ice axe* on another.

axel/axil/axle An *axel* is a jump in figure skating; an *axil* is part of a plant; and an *axle* supports the wheels of a vehicle.

B

Bachmann knot a friction knot.

backcast (v.)

backcountry (n., adj.) In National Park Service terminology, *backcountry* refers specifically to areas not accessible by vehicles. Can also refer generally to wilderness areas, parks, and other places where outdoor recreational activities such as hiking take place. See **frontcountry**.

Back Country Byway a byway designated under the Bureau of Land Management's National Back Country Byway Program. *Back country* is two words in this case.

backcountry horseman Use **trail rider** instead, unless the term appears as part of the name of an organization.

backpack (n., v.) as a verb, means to hike and camp for one or more nights.

backpedal (v.), **backpedaling**

back roads

backup (n., adj.) as in a *backup* plan. Not hyphenated.

back up (v.) two words.

backward not *backwards.*

backwash (n.)

backwater (n.)

backwoods (pl. n., adj.) can take a singular or a plural verb.

back yard (n.), **backyard** (adj.)

badger, badgers, cub

badlands a region nearly devoid of vegetation where erosion has cut the land into a maze of ravines and pinnacles. Almost always used in plural. When capitalized, *Badlands* refers to the area in South Dakota and Nebraska.

Badwater This site in Death Valley is the lowest point in North America, 282 feet below sea level.

Baedeker the guidebook series, published since the 1800s.

-bag One word: *drybag, sandbag.* Two words: *chalk bag, rope bag.*

baitfish (n.) fish used as bait to catch other fish.

bait shop

balaclava a combination hood and face mask; not *Balaklava,* the place in Ukraine.

bald cypress

bald eagle

Band-Aid a trademark; use *adhesive bandage* generally.

bandanna not *bandana.*

Bandelier as in *Bandelier National Monument* (often misspelled *Bandalier*), a park named for Adolph Bandelier (1840–1914), archaeologist and author of *The Delight Makers.* Not *bandolier,* a belt worn across the chest to carry cartridges.

banding in a birding context, this term alone is sufficient; not *bird banding.*

bank the edge of a stream, creek, or river. Lakes and oceans have *shores.*

Bannack, Bannock *Bannack* is a ghost town in Montana, now included in Bannack State Park. *Bannock* is the name of a county and mountain range in Idaho, and also the name of an Indian tribe. Lowercase, *bannock* is a kind of bread (*bannock bread* is redundant).

barbecue (n., v.) not *barbeque* or *Bar-B-Q*, except in some proper names.

barbed wire not *barb wire* or *barbwire*.

barn-door (v.), **barn-dooring** to swing away from the rock face in climbing.

barrel a *double-barreled* shotgun.

barrel racing no hyphen.

barrier-free access Do not use *accessible to the handicapped*, but *wheelchair accessible* is acceptable. See **disability**.

barrier island, barrier reef

Bartram, William (1739–1823) American botanist, author of account of travels through southeastern United States.

basal/basil *Basal* refers to the base of a plant. The herb is *basil* (and *Basel* is the city in Switzerland).

base camp (n.)

BASE jumping The acronym *BASE* stands for *building, antenna, span,* and *earth,* the things from which a BASE jump (with a parachute) may be made.

bashy, bashies a kind of malleable hardware used in extreme aid climbing.

basin Capitalize when part of a proper name of a geologically distinct area: *Great Basin, Powder River Basin.* (Also see **cirque**.) Capitalize in the geological term, *Basin and Range province.*

Lowercase *basin* when referring to an area drained by a river system or the basin of a bay: *the Amazon basin, the Apalachicola Bay basin.*

Basketmaker preferred over *Basket Maker* when referring to the stage of Anasazi culture. Specific stages of classification use roman numerals: *Basketmaker II, Basketmaker III.*

bass (sing., pl.) acceptable second reference for *smallmouth bass* or *largemouth bass* if only one species is being discussed.

bat

bateau, bateaux a kind of flat-bottomed boat.

bathing suit but **swimsuit**.

battles and battlefields Capitalize *battlefield* when it is part of the name of an administrative unit: *the Big Hole National Battlefield.* Lowercase otherwise: *the Big Hole battlefield, the battlefield.* The word *battle* should generally be lowercase: the *battle* of the Big Hole. (If the decision is made to capitalize *battle* in such cases, it should be consistent throughout the text.)

bay Capitalize when part of a proper name: *San Francisco Bay, Bay of Fundy,* but *the bay.* Follow local usage for capitalization of the term *bay area: the San Francisco Bay Area, the Bay Area.*

bay- *Bayfront* and *bayshore* are written as one word, consistent with *waterfront, beachfront,* and *seashore.*

B.C. Small caps, with periods, no spaces between the elements. Follows the year: *1500 B.C.* Note the comma in *11,000 B.C.* Also see A.D., B.C.E., C.E.

B.C.E. stands for "before the common era." Equivalent term to B.C.

beach Capitalize when part of a proper name: *San Gregorio State Beach, Stinson Beach,* but *the beach.* Lowercase when used as a descriptive term: *the Point Reyes beaches.*

beachcomber, beachcombing

beachfront (n., adj.)

beach grass

beach plum

beak and **bill** are synonyms when referring to birds.

beak, birdbeak a kind of piton.

bear, bears, boar, sow, cub

bear bag

bear grass

bear-proof (adj.)

bear spray (n.) or **pepper spray**. The active ingredient is **oleoresin capsicum**.

beaver, beavers, kit

Beckwourth, Jim (1798–1867) mountain man.

-bed Compound nouns with *bed* are generally written as one word: *creekbed, riverbed, roadbed*.

bed-and-breakfast (n., adj.) not *B&B*.

bedroll (n.)

beef The plural form *beeves* appears in contexts referring to cattle as meat. Use *beefs*, however, if you have a lot of complaints.

beetle an insect; not *Beatle* (John, Paul, George, or Ringo).

belay (v., n.), **belayer** (n.) One can be *on belay*. Two words for compound nouns like *belay anchor, belay plate*.

Belize country in Central America; formerly British Honduras. The country of Honduras is to the south.

belt Capitalize in the name of a region: *Sun Belt*.

bench a level area of land, sometimes marking a former shoreline. When used as a geological term, lowercase, consistent with the style for **formations**. When part of a place name, may be capitalized according to local usage.

bergschrund (n.) a crevasse formed where a glacier moves away from a stable area of snow or ice.

Bering Sea, Bering Strait, Bering land bridge

berm preferred over *berme*.

-berry Compound nouns with *berry* are generally written as one word: *cloudberry, huckleberry, serviceberry*. Exception: *buffalo berry*.

beside/besides *beside* means "at the side of," *besides* means "in addition to."

best Hyphenate a compound adjective with *best* before a noun: one of the *best-known* places. No hyphen after the noun: This lake is *best known* for trout.

best-loved (adj.)

best seller (n.), **best-selling** (adj.)

beta information about a climbing route; the term is also used in other sports such as mountain biking.

between/among Use *between* when referring to two things: "I stood *between* my parents." (Never use *among* when referring to only two things.)

Also use *between* when referring to more than two things, considered as individual things: "The marmot sat *between* the rocks." Use *among* for three or more things, considered as a group: "Butterflies swarm *among* the branches." "*Among* your choices are guidebooks for day hikes, backpacking, and scenic driving."

bi- Compounds with *bi* are written as one word (no hyphen): *biweekly, bimonthly.* Note: *biweekly* means every two weeks, not twice a week. To avoid ambiguity, write *twice a week* or *twice a month.*

Bierstadt, Albert (1830–1902) American landscape painter, born in Germany, known for paintings of the Rocky Mountains and Yellowstone National Park.

big compound nouns using *big* are generally open: *big wall, big water, big wave.* Hyphenate the adjective forms: *big-wall climbing, big-wave surfing.*

Bigfoot or **Sasquatch**

Big Four Charles Crocker, Mark Hopkins, Collis P. Huntington, and Leland Stanford.

big game (n.), **big-game** (adj.)

bighorn sheep (sing., pl.), ram, ewe, lamb The short form *bighorn* is okay on second reference.

Bighorn, Big Horn *Bighorn Mountains* and *Bighorn River* in Montana and Wyoming. (USGS actually has *Big Horn Mountains*, Montana, and *Bighorn Mountains*, Wyoming; for consistency, write as one word.) Also: *Big Horn County* in Montana and Wyoming. *Bighorn Canyon*, Wyoming. The town of *Big Horn*, Wyoming.

bight a loop of rope, as in "take a *bight* of rope." Can also mean a bend in a shoreline, or the bay formed in such a bend. Not to be confused with *bite*.

the Big Island the island of Hawaii.

bigleaf maple

bigtooth maple

bilge pump (n.)

billfish (n.)

Billy the Kid *the Kid* okay on second reference. Also known as Henry McCarty or **William H. Bonney.**

bio- Compounds with *bio* are written as one word (no hyphen): *biodegradable, biodiversity, biogeography, biomass, biosolids, biosphere.*

Biosphere Reserve Capitalize this designation of UNESCO's Man and the Biosphere Program. In the United States, a number of national parks have been designated Biosphere Reserves. Not *International Biosphere Reserve* or *World Biosphere Reserve*.

birch bark (n.), **birch-bark** (adj.)

bird (generally), **birds, nestling** (before it leaves the nest), **fledgling** (after it leaves the nest) Compound nouns with *bird* are usually written as separate words when referring to general kinds of birds: *birds of prey, field birds.*

birdbeak a piton originally made by A5 Adventures. Now used generically, so lowercase.

birdcall (n.)

bird dog (n.), **bird-dog** (v.)

birder (n.) *bird watcher* also acceptable, not *bird-watcher.*

birding (n.) *bird watching* also acceptable, not *bird-watching:* We are going *birding.*

bird names Lowercase except for words that are proper nouns: *common loon, Pacific loon.* Bird names also follow the standard rule on apostrophes: *Ross's goose.*

Rules for a field guide in which bird names are capitalized: in a two-word name, both words are capitalized: *Snowy Owl.* In a hyphenated term, the second word is usually lowercase: *Long-eared Owl.*

bird of prey (n.) no hyphen. Plural: *birds of prey.*

bird's-eye (adj.) as in a *bird's-eye view.*

bird-watching (adj.) a *bird-watching* guide, not a *birding* guide.

birthday Capitalize in the name of an official holiday: The event takes place on *Washington's Birthday.* Lowercase if it is not an official holiday: a lecture held on *Thoreau's birthday.* Also see **holidays.**

bison (sing., pl.), bull, cow, calf *bison* preferred over **buffalo** except in historical references. The scientific name is *Bison bison. Buffalo* okay when referring to food: *buffalo burgers.*

bitterbrush

bitterroot one word, in the plant name or place names: *Bitterroot Valley, Bitterroot Mountains.* These place names may, however, appear as two words in historical references, such as titles of older books.

bivouac (n., v.), **bivouacked, bivouacking**

bivy sack (n.) a one-person shelter, smaller than a tent.

Black capitalize when referring to **African Americans.**

black-and-white (adj.)

black bear regardless of color. To describe a different color, write *cinnamon-colored black bear, brown-phase black bear,* etc.

Blackfeet when referring to American (specifically Montanan) members of the Blackfoot Confederacy. *Blackfoot* refers to the entire Confederacy, which includes tribes in Canada.

black fly

Blackfoot the river in Montana. Also see **Blackfeet.**

Black Hills

black ice

Blackrobes an Indian term for Jesuit priests in the West.

black-tailed deer not *blacktail deer.*

black-tailed prairie dog

blaze (n.) an ax mark on a tree designating a trail (one of the most typical resembles a lowercase letter "i").

BLM, Bureau of Land Management

blowdown (n.)

blowhole (n.)

blowsand, blowsand desert, blowsand dunes refers to wind-blown sand, as found, for example, in the California desert.

bluefish

bluegill

bluegrass preferred over *blue grass.* Capitalize *Bluegrass Country* or *Bluegrass Region,* Kentucky.

bluestem (n.)

blue water (n.), **bluewater** (adj.) deep offshore waters in the Atlantic. *BlueWater* for the company that makes climbing ropes.

bluff charge (n.), **bluff-charge** (v.) The grizzly *bluff-charged* me twice.

boar, boars, piglet

board feet (collective n.) takes a singular verb: A million *board feet was* harvested in 1922.

boardsailing (n.) The term **sailboarding** is preferred.

boardwalk

boat names See **ship names**.

bobcat, bobcats, kitten

Bodmer, Karl (1809–1893) painter known for portraits of Indians.

bodysurf (v.)

bog (n.) a waterlogged area, the ground often consisting of peat. Compare **marsh, swamp**.

bombproof (adj.) as in a *bombproof* placement. Not *bomb-proof.*

bone-dry (adj.)

bonefish

Bonney, William H. (1859?–1881) Also known as Henry McCarty. **Billy the Kid,** who was shot by Pat Garrett.

book signing (n.), **book-signing** (adj.)

boomtown

bootlace

boreal (adj.) relating to northern regions. Capitalized, refers specifically to certain northern forest areas. Not **arboreal,** relating to trees.

Bosch drill used to drill holes for bolts in climbing.

bosun a variant of *boatswain,* common in a nautical context: *bosun's chair.*

bota

bottomland(s) low-lying land along a river. Also see **-land.**

boulder (v.), **bouldering** (n.)

boulder field (n.)

bound In compounds with a compass direction, write as one word: *northbound, southbound.* In compounds with a place, hyphenate: *Canada-bound, desert-bound.* Use an en dash, not a hyphen, when combining with a two-word place name: *Grand Canyon–bound.*

bowhunter

bowie knife lowercase. Named for frontiersman Jim Bowie.

box canyon (n.)

Boy Scouts Use the full name, *Boy Scouts of America,* on first reference. *Scouts* (capital "s") is acceptable on second reference if it is clear that what is being discussed is Boy Scouts only, not another organization like **Girl Scouts of the United States of America.**

bracken (n.)/**brackish** (adj.) *Bracken* is a kind of fern, or an area overgrown with this fern. *Brackish* water is salty: a *brackish* lagoon.

Brady, Mathew B. (1823–1896) Civil War photographer. Not *Matthew.*

break in (v.), **break-in** (n.)

breaks (n.) broken land at the border of an upland that is crisscrossed with ravines; capitalize in a proper name: *Cedar Breaks, the Missouri Breaks.*

breakup (n.) *spring breakup* (when ice melts).

break up (v.)

breakwater (n.)

breathtaking (adj.)

bridal/bridle *Bridal* is an adjective referring to a bride. *Bridle* is a noun referring to part of a horse's harness and can be used as an adjective: *a bridle path, bridle leather.*

bridge Capitalize when part of a proper noun: *Golden Gate Bridge,* but *the bridge.* Natural bridges are also capitalized: *Kachina Bridge* at Natural Bridges National Monument. If the bridge is unnamed, or if the term is used descriptively, as for a **railroad bridge,** lowercase: *the Mill Creek bridge.*

Bridger, Jim (1804–1881) mountain man.

-brim *a wide-brimmed hat* preferred over *a wide-brim hat.*

bristlecone pine

British/Canadian spellings and usage Avoid British spellings such as *grey, theatre, catalogue,* and so on, unless they are part of a proper name or unless the writing is intended for a Canadian or British readership.

Also avoid British usages such as *abseil* for *rappel.*

British Honduras called **Belize** since 1973.

bronco, bronc a wild or unbroken horse; also called a **mustang.**

brook trout Use *Eastern brook trout* on first reference; *brookies* is acceptable on second reference.

Brooks Range (Alaska)

brown bear a subspecies of **grizzly bear** found in coastal areas of Alaska.

brown trout On second reference, *browns* is acceptable.

-brush Compound nouns with *brush* are usually written as one word: *bitterbrush, rabbitbrush, sagebrush.*

brushfire preferred over *brush fire.*

bucket hold, bucket a rock climbing term.

buckshot is large-size shot; the terms *buckshot* and *shot* are not interchangeable.

buffalo Use **bison** except in historical references and when referring to food.

buffalo berry two words; an exception to the general rule for **berry.**

Buffalo Bill See **Cody, William F.**

Buffalo Bill Historical Center in Cody, Wyoming, includes four museums: Buffalo Bill Museum, Cody Firearms Museum, Plains Indian Museum, and Whitney Gallery of Western Art.

buffalo robe

buildering like **bouldering,** but climbing on buildings.

building If a building is a landmark or otherwise considered a destination for visitors, and *building* is commonly considered part of the name, then capitalize the word: *Empire State Building.* Lowercase when merely a descriptive term. Note that the term *capitol building* is redundant; a capitol is a building.

In general, capitalize the names of institutional buildings such as churches, libraries, museums, and schools. Also capitalize the names of buildings that are historic sites and/or destinations for visitors and managed as such: *Scotty's Castle, the Palace of the Governors, the Robert Louis Stevenson House.* See further discussion at **home.**

bunch grass

bungee, bungee cord not *bungi.*

bunkhouse

bunny hop (v.) the mountain biking maneuver.

buoy (n., v.)

bur preferred when referring to a prickly kind of seed. People from Scotland may speak with a *burr.*

Bureau of Land Management, BLM Note: Capitalize the names of BLM resource areas: *the San Juan Resource Area.*

bureau of land reclamation There is no such agency. Either *Bureau of Land Management* or *Bureau of Reclamation.*

burned/burnt *Burned* generally preferred as a past participle: Twenty acres were *burned* in the fire. *Burnt* may be preferred as an adjective (*burnt* offering). Let your ear be the judge.

burro a donkey. Lowercase the words *jack*, for a male, and *jenny*, for a female (plural *jennies*).

Burroughs, John (1837–1921) naturalist and writer.

bus, buses

bush pilot (n.)

bushwhack (v.) to travel through dense undergrowth or otherwise hike without a trail.

butte an isolated hill or small mountain, especially one with steep sides and a flat top, usually smaller than a **mesa.**

buttress Capitalize when commonly accepted as part of the name of a mountain feature, as in the names of many climbing routes: *the West Buttress.*

buzzbait lowercase; a kind of lure.

byway (n.) Also see **Back Country Byway, National Scenic Byway,** and **scenic byway.**

C

Cabela's, Inc. the outdoor products store.

cache/cash A *cache* is a hiding place or the things stored there. Also a verb: They plan to *cache* food for the return trip. *Cash* is money.

cactus *Cacti* preferred over *cactuses* for plural.

caddis fly

cafe no accent.

cagoule a style of rain jacket with an adjustable hemline.

Cahokia Mounds an archaeological site in Illinois. Capitalize the names of individual mounds: *Monks Mound.*

cairn (n.), **cairned** (adj.) a *cairned* trail.

Cajun originally "Acadian."

Calamity Jane (1852?–1903) Her real name was Martha Jane Canary. Her last name is also sometimes given as Burk or Burke.

caldera a large, basin-shaped volcanic depression, many times greater in size than the volcanic vent or vents it contains. Lowercase: *the Yellowstone caldera.*

calf roping no hyphen.

caliber the diameter of the inside of a gun barrel, measured in millimeters (*a 9 mm pistol*) or in decimal fractions of an inch (*a .22-caliber rifle, a .45-caliber revolver*). Note that there is no hyphen when caliber is given in millimeters; there is a hyphen with decimal fractions of an inch.

caliche A road surface consisting of hard earth or clay. Also known as **hardpan.**

callous (adj.)/**callus** (n.) *Callous* means "insensitive"; a *callus* is a patch of thickened, hardened skin. A hiker's feet might be *callused*. *Calloused* is not a word.

Calvary/cavalry *Calvary* was the site of the Crucifixion; **cavalry** is a military unit on horseback.

calve (v.), **calving** creation of icebergs when pieces break off glaciers.

cam, camming device

Camalot trade name for a spring-loaded camming device made by Black Diamond (not *Camelot*, land of King Arthur).

camas preferred over *camass*. Spellings of place names may vary.

camcorder (n.)

CamelBak a brand of hydration pack (not *Camelback*, the Arizona place name).

camouflage

camp One word: *campfire, campground, campsite.* Two words: *tent site.*

campground Write the names of campgrounds according to the usage of the managing agency: *Gallo Campground* at Chaco Culture National Historical Park, *Sky Camp* at Point Reyes. Spell out the number in *Camp Four,* Yosemite.

Canada Provinces, with postal abbreviations: Alberta (AB), British Columbia (BC), Manitoba (MB), New Brunswick (NB), Newfoundland (NF), Nova Scotia (NS), Ontario (ON), Prince Edward Island (PE), Quebec (QC), and Saskatchewan (SK). Territories: Yukon Territory (YT), Northwest Territories (NT), and, beginning in 1999, Nunavut Territory (also NT).

Canada goose, Canada geese never *Canadian* goose/geese.

Canadian Permanent Committee on Geographical Names

Canadian Rockies the mountain ranges along the Continental Divide north of the U.S. border, bounded on the west by the east side of the Columbia Valley Trench (source: Banff National Park).

Canadian Ski Patrol System

Canadian Wildlife Service (CWS) part of Environment Canada.

canal Capitalize when part of a proper name: *Panama Canal, Erie Canal,* but *the canal* on second reference.

canoe, canoeing, canoeist

cañon Use **canyon** except in certain historical references.

Canuck an offensive term; use **French Canadian.**

canyon not **cañon.** Capitalize when part of a proper name: *Arch Canyon, the Grand Canyon,* but *the canyon.*

canyonland(s) can refer generally to canyon-dominated areas in the Southwest/Four Corners region. Capitalize *Canyonlands* only when referring specifically to Canyonlands National Park in Utah.

cape Capitalize when part of a proper name: *Cape Cod,* but *the cape.*

Capilene a trademark of Patagonia.

capital/capitol Use *capital* to refer to a city, *capitol* to refer to a building. *Capitol building* is, thus, redundant. The national park in Utah is *Capitol Reef.*

caprock

carabiner, 'biner, or **biner** *bent-gate carabiner, D carabiner, locking carabiner.*

carbon dating (n.), **carbon-date** (v.)

carbon-14

Carhartt the manufacturer of work clothing.

Caribbean

Cariboo Mountains, the Cariboos the mountain range in British Columbia; not **caribou,** the animal.

caribou (sing., pl.), bull, cow, calf

cartridge contains a bullet; fired by a rifle or pistol. Shotguns use shells filled with shot.

cash/cache See usage note at **cache/cash.**

cast (v.) *backcast, false cast, roll cast.*

catalog not *catalogue.*

catamaran

cataraft

catch-and-release (n., adj.)

catch fire not *catch on fire.*

cat hole

Catlin, George (1796–1872) American artist known for portraits of Indians.

cattail

cattleguard (n.)

cattleman Use *rancher* for a nonsexist alternative.

Caucasian Use **White** or **Anglo-American** or **Anglo.**

cavalry/Calvary See usage note at **Calvary/cavalry.**

cave in (v.), **cave-in** (n.)

cave/cavern The terms can be interchangeable, although a cavern usually is a large cave, or one chamber of a cave. Capitalize when part of a proper name: *Mummy Cave, Carlsbad Caverns.*

cavers, caving preferred to **spelunkers, spelunking.**

cay a small, low island of coral or sand; usually **key** in the Gulf of Mexico, as in the *Florida Keys.* Not **quay,** a wharf.

CB, CB radio short for *citizens band, citizens band radio.* No apostrophe in *citizens.*

C.E. Stands for "common era." Equivalent term to A.D.

cellular phone, cell phone

Celsius not *centigrade.* In text, use the abbreviation *C* (no period): *20 degrees C.* Use **Fahrenheit** temperatures in books for a U.S. audience.

central Lowercase before the name of a city: *central Houston.*

Central Flyway

century Spell out, and lowercase: *twentieth century* (n.). Hyphenate the adjective form: *a nineteenth-century map.*

cerro means "peak," as in *Cerro Torre* in Argentina.

cfs cubic feet per second; used to measure the flow of a river.

Chaco Culture National Historical Park *Chaco Canyon* acceptable on second reference.

chain saw (n.), **chain-saw** (v.)

chairlift

chalet Capitalize when part of the proper name of a building: *Granite Park Chalet*, but *the chalet*.

chalk bag

chamber of commerce Lowercase when used alone: Contact the *chamber of commerce* for more information. Capitalize with a place name, but note that some chambers of commerce have names other than simply the name of the town.

chamois the European antelope; also the leather or cloth.

Champlain, Samuel de (1567?–1635) French explorer; one of the founders of Quebec.

channel Capitalize when part of a proper name: *the English Channel*, but *the channel*.

Channel Islands off the coast of Southern California; also the British islands in the English Channel.

chaparral

ChapStick a trademark; for a general term, use *lip balm*.

cheater stick

cheatgrass

checklist one word except in the title *Check-list of North American Birds* published by the American Ornithologists' Union.

Chetro Ketl a ruin at Chaco Canyon; not *Kettle*.

Cheyenne the capital of Wyoming; the *Cheyenne River*, in Wyoming and South Dakota. Note: The river in North Dakota is the *Sheyenne River*.

Chicano, Chicana refer specifically to an American of Mexican heritage. See **Hispanic**.

chickee Seminole Indian open-air hut, built on a platform, with a thatched roof.

chickenhead a climbing hold of about that size.

Chief Joseph (1840?–1904) the Nez Perce leader.

chile/Chile/chili Use *chile* for the pepper. *Chile* is the South American country, and *chili* is the dish.

chimney in climbing, a crack more than 8-inches wide. See also **hand jam** and **off-width crack**.

Chinese American (n.) Hyphenate when used as an adjective.

chinook/Chinook Lowercase when referring to the wind; capitalize when referring to the people or their language.

Chinook salmon

chipmunk, chipmunks

chock a nut or wedge. All are generic terms and thus lowercase.

chokeberry, chokecherry not the same plant.

cholla a kind of cactus.

Chouinard, Yvon (1938–) climber; founder of the companies Chouinard Equipment (now called Black Diamond) and Patagonia.

christie turn not *Christie turn*.

Christmas Bird Count conducted by the National Audubon Society.

chuck wagon

chuckwalla

chuck-will's-widow Note the hyphens.

chugger lowercase; a kind of lure.

chukar/chukka A *chukar* is a kind of partridge; a *chukka* is a low boot.

chum (n., v.) bait spread on water; or to attract fish by spreading bait.

chunnel the tunnel below the English Channel; lowercase.

church Capitalize the name of an individual building. Also capitalize when referring to an organized religion: *the Catholic Church.* Lowercase when used alone: *St. John's is a Catholic church.*

Church, Frederick (1826–1900) painter of the Hudson River school.

Church of Jesus Christ of Latter-day Saints the formal name of the Mormon Church.

chute/shoot A *chute* is a rapid or waterfall; but one *shoots* rapids.

Cíbola, Cibola There is an accent in *Cíbola,* the mythical land sought by Coronado in the Southwest. No accent in the spellings of New Mexico place names: *Cibola County, Cibola National Forest.*

cienaga, cienega marshy land, in the Southwest; use the spelling most common in the region.

cinder cone (n.)

circle Capitalize in *the Arctic Circle.*

circlehead(s) climbing gear.

circum- Compounds with this prefix, which means "around" or "about," are written as one word: *circumboreal, circumnavigate, circumpolar.*

cirque a hollow at the upper part of a mountain valley, usually glacier-carved and often containing a lake. In the Rocky Mountains, cirques are known as *basins.*

Cities Capitalize in place names such as *Tri-Cities* (Washington), *Twin Cities* (Minnesota), *Quad Cities* (Illinois and Iowa).

city Capitalize when part of the name: *Virginia City.* Lowercase when the word appears before the name: *the city of Helena.* Exception: may be capitalized when referring to the city as a corporate body as in *the City of Helena passed the ordinance.* Also note the capitalization of place names such as *City of Rocks,* the climbing area in Idaho.

city hall Capitalize when used with a city name or if reference is specific (not general, as in "you can't fight *city hall*").

Civil War *the war* on second reference. Note the en dash in the compound adjective: *a Civil War–era gun.*

Civilian Conservation Corps, CCC

clamshell

Clark, William (1770–1838) Leader, with Meriwether Lewis, of the Lewis and Clark Expedition.

class III river the form of a rafting designation. The word *class* is lowercase; use roman numerals except for class 5. Ratings: class I, class II, class II+, class III-, class III, class III+, class IV-, class IV, class IV+. In class 5, arabic numerals are used to allow for open-ended decimal gradations of difficulty: for example, *class 5.2.* Class VI is reserved for extreme, possibly unrunnable rivers; once such a river has been run, it is likely to be given a class 5 rating of some kind.

class 5 climb climbing designation. Ratings go from class I (trail hiking) to class 5 (ropes and protection needed). The word *class* is lower case; use arabic numerals.

The **Yosemite Decimal System** is used to rate class 5 climbs in the form 5.3 to 5.14. For grades of 5.10 and greater, lowercase letters are used to indicate additional gradations: *5.12a.* See further discussion at **aid climbing.** Also see *Mountaineering: The Freedom of the Hills,* listed in **For Further Reference,** for detailed discussions of the Yosemite Decimal System and other international rating systems.

Clean Air Act (1970)

Clean Water Act popular name for the formal title, the Federal Water Pollution Control Act (Amendments of 1972).

clearcut (n., v., adj.) referring to the logging practice. Note: hyphenate *clear-cut* (adj.) when the meaning is "distinct," as in a *clear-cut* solution.

clevis pin (n.)

Clif Bar

cliff Capitalize when part of a name: *the Book Cliffs, the cliffs.* Lowercase when used as a descriptive term.

Cliff Dweller an outdated term. Use **Anasazi** or **Ancestral Pueblo(an)** instead. The term *cliff dwelling* is okay to describe ruins: the *cliff dwellings* at Mesa Verde.

climactic/climatic *Climactic* refers to a climax, *climatic* refers to climate.

climbing gear Capitalize trademarks and brand names of specific products. See individual entries.

climbing route names are capitalized and set in roman type.

cling hold(s) (n.)

clip in (v.)

close-up (n., adj., adv.)

cloud Lowercase kinds of clouds: *altocumulus, altostratus, cirrocumulus, cirrostratus, cirrus, cumulonimbus, cumulus, nimbostratus, stratocumulus, stratus.*

cloudburst (n.)

cloud forest

coalfield (n.)

coaming (n.) a rim such as that around the opening of a kayak.

coast Capitalize *West Coast, East Coast, Gulf Coast,* as names of regions. Lowercase when used as a descriptive term referring to an actual coastline: *beaches along the California coast.*

Coast Guard *the U.S. Coast Guard, the Coast Guard.* Also see **armed forces.**

coastline

Coast Ranges include the mountains along the Pacific coast from California north to Alaska. In California, often used in the singular.

coati, coatis an omnivorous mammal resembling a raccoon.

cod, cod *cods* if referring to more than one species.

Cody, William F. (1846–1917) Also known as **Buffalo Bill.** The name of his show was *Buffalo Bill's Wild West* (no *Show* at the end of this name).

coffeepot

coho salmon *cohos* acceptable on second reference.

col a mountain pass between peaks, also known as a **saddle**. Not **couloir**, a mountain gorge or gully. Capitalize when part of a proper name: the *North Col.*

coldwater (adj.) one word when used to characterize a river or stream as trout habitat; used for all Trout Unlimited publications: "The Yellowstone River is an outstanding *coldwater* fishery."

cold wave (n.)

Coleman the outdoor products manufacturer.

collapsible (adj.) preferred over *collapsable.*

collared peccary a piglike mammal of the desert southwest also called javelina.

colonial (adj.) but *the Colonies.* Lowercase the adjective *colonial* when used in a general sense, referring to the architectural style. Capitalize when referring to buildings that actually date from the Colonial period.

Colorado Plateau

Colt Capitalize when naming the kind of gun: *a Colt .45-caliber revolver.*

common names (of plants, animals) See **animal names, plant names,** and so on. For scientific names, see **taxonomy.**

common sense (n.), **commonsense** (adj.)

commonwealth The states that are commonwealths are Kentucky, Massachusetts, Pennsylvania, and Virginia. Lowercase the *commonwealth* of Virginia, just like the *state* of Georgia. It is fine to refer to the *state of Virginia;* the term *commonwealth* is needed only when referring to one of these states as a legal entity.

compose/comprise Parts *compose* a whole, and a whole *comprises* its parts. Fifty-six counties *compose* the state of Montana, but Montana *comprises* fifty-six counties.

compound leaf

Concord coach a kind of stagecoach built by the Abbot-Downing Company of Concord, New Hampshire.

coneflower

Conestoga wagon a covered wagon.

constellations Capitalize their names: *the Big Dipper, Orion.* Also capitalize *the Milky Way.*

contiguous (adj.) connected or touching: *contiguous* states.

continent, continental Lowercase, as in the *continent* of North America. Capitalized, *the Continent* and *Continental* mean "Europe" and "European."

Continental Divide Use *divide* (lowercase) in subsequent references.

continental shelf, continental slope lowercase.

continuous/continual *Continuous* means ongoing without interruption: a *continuous* trail. *Continual* means recurring: the *continual* noise of birds.

contour (v.) A verb that takes an object: engineers *contoured* the road. *Contour* is sometimes used intransitively (the trail *contours* along the hillside), but it is better to reword: *the trail hugs the hillside, the trail follows the contours of the hillside.*

Convention on Wetlands of International Importance also known as the **Ramsar Convention.**

Cooper, James Fenimore (1789–1851) author of *The Last of the Mohicans* and other novels.

copperhead, c-head

Copper King(s) Capitalize when referring to Marcus Daly and William A. Clark, owners of Montana copper mines.

coprolite fossilized dung.

cordelette

cord grass

cordillera in Central or South America, a mountain range.

Cordura a trademark.

Corinne town in Utah; not *Corrinne.*

Corn Belt

Coronado, Francisco Vásquez de (1510–1554) Spanish explorer of the Southwest.

Corps of Discovery another term for the **Lewis and Clark Expedition.**

Corps of Topographical Engineers from 1838 to 1863, a unit of the federal government that conducted surveys of the West. Not the same as the *Corps of Engineers,* with which it merged in 1863.

Cortez, Sea of

Cotton Belt

coulee a ravine; term used almost exclusively in the western United States.

couloir a mountain gorge or gully. Compare **col.**

countryside (n.)

county Capitalize following the name: *Ravalli County.* Lowercase before the name: *the county of Spokane.* Note: The *GPO Style Manual* (see **For Further Reference**) has a list of U.S. counties by state and a list of similar county names that are spelled differently in different states.

couple of *A couple of* is correct: "The trail forks after *a couple of* miles," not "The trail forks after *a couple* miles." *A couple* may be appropriate, however, in informal, quoted speech.

covey a flock of quail or partridge.

cow, cows, bull (*steer* is neutered), **cow** (*heifer* is a young cow that hasn't yet given birth), **calf**

cowpat

cowpath

cow town

coyote, coyotes, pup

coypu another name for **nutria.**

Cracker a term for a poor White Southerner, usually (although not always) considered offensive. Do not use.

crampon(s) (n.) can also be used as a verb: "We *cramponed* up the slope."

crane fly

crankbait

crappie, crappies

crash pad a mat used to cushion a fall in bouldering.

Crazy Horse (1842?–1877) Sioux leader. The year of his birth is given as 1841, 1842, or 1849 in various reference books.

The Crazy Horse Memorial, begun by sculptor **Korczak Ziolkowski,** is being carved in the Black Hills of South Dakota.

creekbed Also *railbed, riverbed, roadbed.*

crenellated/crenulated *Crenellated* refers to battlements, as on a castle. *Crenulated* refers to a wavy or serrated edge; a leaf can be *crenulated.*

creosote bush

crevasse/crevice A *crevasse* is a deep vertical fissure in a glacier. A *crevice* is any narrow crack, as in a cliff.

crisscross (v.) Trails *crisscross* the park.

Crockett, Davy (1786–1836) not *Davey.*

crossbow (n.)

cross-country (adj., adv.) Do not use *XC* as an abbreviation.

cross-country skiing (n.) a type of **Nordic skiing.**

crossroads one word, but may occasionally appear as two words in a place name: *Brices Cross Roads National Battlefield Site.*

cross section (n.) or **cross-section** author's preference, but should be consistent.

crux (n.) the most difficult part of a climb.

cryptobiotic soil/crust a fragile blend of living mosses, lichens, and bacteria, typically found in desert/arid areas.

cryptogam, cryptogamic crust another term for **cryptobiotic soil/crust.** Not *cryptogram,* a cipher.

crystal clear (adj.) Hyphenate before a noun: *a crystal-clear stream.* No need to hyphenate after the noun.

Cub Scout(s)

cul-de-sac a dead-end street. No need to italicize. Plural: *culs-de-sac* or *cul-de-sacs,* based on author's preference; just be consistent.

currant / current *Currant* is the shrub or berry; *current* refers to running water.

Curtis, Edward Sheriff (1868–1952) photographer known for his portraits of American Indians.

Custer, George Armstrong (1839–1876) *Lieutenant Colonel George Armstrong Custer*, not *General Custer*. (The latter was a brevet rank he was given during the Civil War. Technically, it was not applicable after the war, although Custer, like many other officers, still retained the title.)

Custer Battlefield Do not use; instead, use *Little Bighorn Battlefield*.

cutbank one word for the geological term, but two words for the town in Montana, *Cut Bank*.

cutoff (n.) preferred over *cut-off.* Capitalize when commonly considered part of the name of a route, especially in historical references: The Donner Party regretted having taken the *Hastings Cutoff.* Pants cut into shorts are also *cutoffs*.

cutthroat trout *cutthroats* or *cutts* acceptable on second reference.

D

daisy chain webbing sling with loops used in aid climbing.

Dall sheep not *Dall's sheep*.

The Dalles (Oregon) with a capital *The*; but *the Dalles region.* Lowercase, *dalles* (pl. n.) are rapids in a rock-walled river gorge.

dams Capitalize when part of a proper name: *Hoover Dam,* but *the dam* on second reference. Lowercase when used descriptively, as for a small, unnamed dam: *the Belmont Creek dam.*

Dardevle a brand of fishing lures made by Eppinger Manufacturing. Also *Seadevle, Devle Dog.*

Darwin, Charles (1809–1882) author of *Origin of Species.*

date line lowercase. Also called the **international date line.** The imaginary line along the 180th meridian. Note: as one word, *dateline* refers to the origin of a news story.

dates Write dates in month-day-year order. In running text, the year should be set off by commas: *She was born on August 10, 1955, in New York.* No comma is used when the date consists of a month and year only: *August 1955.*

Years: *1960,* not *'60.* Decades: *1960s,* not *1960's* or *the sixties.* Spell out terms like *Roaring Twenties.* Centuries are always spelled out: *the end of the twentieth century; a twentieth-century invention.* Link a range of years with an en dash, and always give the full year: *1960–1970,* not *1960–70.*

Avoid beginning a sentence with a year, because it must then be spelled out. Instead of *"Nineteen eighty-nine was a year of drought,"* rewrite as *"There was a drought in 1989."*

Dawes Act or **General Allotment Act** (1887) allotted lands to Indians, leaving the remainder open to settlement by Whites. The full name is the *Dawes Severalty Act,* but it is commonly referred to by the shorter name.

day One word: *daybreak, daylight, daytime.*

day hike

daylight-saving time preferred over *daylight time.*

day pack (n.) smaller than a frame pack, and used for day trips.

day trip (n.), **day-tripper** (n.)

day use area

DDT the insecticide; okay on first reference.

dead end (n.), **dead-end** (v., adj.)

deadfall (n.) fallen trees and branches, for example strewn across a trail. Sometimes *downfall.*

Dead Horse Point State Park a Utah state park, adjacent to Canyonlands National Park.

Death Valley National Park no longer a national monument.

debark/disembark *disembark* preferred to describe leaving a ship.

decades No apostrophe, and give the full date: *1890s, 1980s, mid-1950s* (not *'50s* or *fifties*). Spell out names of decades, such as *Roaring Twenties.*

-deep Compound adjectives with *deep* are usually written with a hyphen: *ankle-deep, skin-deep, waist-deep.*

deep-sea (adj.)

Deep South

deep water (n.) As adjective, *deep-water* is preferred over *deepwater.*

deer (sing., pl.), **buck, doe, fawn**

deer hunting season

Deer Lodge two words for the county and town in Montana; one word in *Deerlodge National Forest.*

deer moss

deer fly preferred over *deerfly.*

Deere in the name of the brand of tractor, *John Deere.*

deet the insect repellent, diethyl toluamide.

degree Use numerals for measurements: *a 360-degree view, a 45-degree slope, a slope of 45 degrees.* Spell out the number when referring to burns: *first-degree burn.*

DeLorme the map publisher based in Maine.

delta area at the mouth of a river. Capitalize when part of the name of a populated region: *Mississippi River Delta, the delta.* (The larger and more populated the area, the more likely it is to be capitalized.) Lowercase when used as a descriptive term, especially when the area is small or not significantly inhabited by people: *Nisqually River delta.*

Denali An alternate name for Mount McKinley, the highest peak in North America (20,320 feet). *Denali* is always used in the name of the park, *Denali National Park and Preserve.* The official name of the peak remains *Mount McKinley* in National Park Service and USGS usage.

depot See **station.**

depression Lowercase in a general sense, but capitalize *Great Depression.*

derailleur (n.)

derring-do (n.)

Deseret appears in Utah place names; refers to area originally intended as a Mormon state. Not *desert,* an arid region.

desert Compound nouns with desert are usually written as two words: *desert rat, desert tortoise, desert varnish.* Also, it is *desert,* not *desserts,* in the expression *just deserts,* meaning you get what you deserve.

desert varnish (n.) the dark coating on cliffs produced by oxidation of minerals such as iron. The word *patina* is more appropriate in areas that are not deserts.

Devils In general, place names with the word *Devils* do not take an apostrophe, except in historical references. Follow the usage as shown on USGS maps: *Devils Postpile National Monument, Devils Tower National Monument.* Do watch for inconsistencies between *Devil* and *Devils*: in California, for example, there is a *Devil Peak* in both Mariposa County and Placer County, as well as a *Devils Peak* in Placer County.

De Voto, Bernard (1897–1955) historian, author of *Across the Wide Missouri.*

dew- One word: *dewclaw, dewdrop, dewlap.* Two words: *dew point.*

dihedral (n.) where two rock walls meet to form a corner; a rock climb may follow a *dihedral.*

Diné or **Dineh** The Navajo people's name for themselves. Either spelling is acceptable; just be consistent.

Dinetah the traditional Navajo homeland, an area of north-western New Mexico.

dinghy a small boat; *dingy* means drab or dirty.

direct aid climbing

directions See **north, south, east,** and **west.** Also see **Maps, Roads, and Directions,** p. 14.

dirt Compound nouns with *dirt* are usually written as two words: *dirt road, dirt bike.* Adjectives are hyphenated: *dirt-cheap, dirt-poor.*

disability, people with disabilities *Disability* is a general term for a functional limitation that interferes with a person's ability, for example, to walk, lift, hear, or learn. It may refer to a physical, sensory, or mental condition. See *Guidelines for Reporting and Writing About People with Disabilities* in **For Further Reference**, and when possible, respect the preferences of the person(s) being discussed. Do not use **handicapped.** Also see the entry under **impairments.**

disassemble/dissemble To *disassemble* is to take apart; to *dissemble* is to disguise or feign, as feelings.

disembark preferred over **debark.**

distances See **mile** and **Maps, Roads, and Directions,** p. 14.

District of Columbia *the District* or *D.C.* (no space between the letters); in the full name *Washington, D.C.,* the letters are set off by commas within a sentence.

diversion ditch a narrow, shallow ditch dug across or around a trail to funnel away water and prevent erosion.

dobsonfly

dock (n.) water between piers or alongside a pier; also a synonym for a wharf or pier.

dogleg (v.) to bend sharply: a road or trail may *dogleg.*

dogsled (n., v.), **dogsledder, dogsledding** but two words for *sled dog.*

Dolly Varden

Donner Party Capitalize, as the name of a historically significant expedition.

doubletrack (n., adj.) a trail or jeep road with two distinct ribbons of walking or riding surface. Also see **singletrack.**

Douglas-fir (n.) not *Douglas fir.*

dove, doves

dowitcher a kind of shore bird; not *dowager,* an old woman.

down- Compounds with *down* are usually written as one word: *downfall, downgrade, downhill, download, downpour, downriver, downshift, downshore, downstream, downwind.*

downclimb (v.)

downcurrent (adj., adv.)

Down East Hancock and Washington Counties, Maine (may also be used to describe parts of Maine beyond these counties). Sometimes *Downeast.* Use the most common spelling in the area being discussed.

downhill skiing a general term; see **alpine** and **Nordic skiing.**

down-home (adj.)

downstate the corresponding term to **upstate.**

Down Under Australia, New Zealand

downwind (n., adj.)

draft not *draught.*

drag (v.) The past tense is *dragged,* not *drug:* The bear *dragged* my pack away.

drainage Lowercase as a descriptive term following a creek or river name.

Dramamine a trademark for an antihistamine used to counteract motion sickness.

drawcord, drawstring

drift Two words: *drift boat, drift net.* One word: *driftwood.*

D-ring

dripstone a stalactite or stalagmite.

drought preferred over *drouth.*

drumlin a hill originally formed beneath a glacier.

drybag

dry dock (n.)

drytop a waterproof jacket used in paddlesports.

duck, ducks, drake, hen, duckling

Duck Stamp The formal name is the *Migratory Bird Hunting and Conservation Stamp.*

duct tape

duffek, duffek stroke

duffle or **duffel** bag or coat; author's preference, but should be consistent.

dugout (n.) canoe or shelter; not *dug-out.*

dugway When part of a road name, capitalize: the *Moki Dugway, the dugway.*

dulfersitz method of rappelling with rope only (no harness).

Dust Bowl Capitalize when referring to the specific environmental conditions of the 1930s. Lowercase if referring generally to a dry, dusty area.

dust devil

dust storm

Dutch oven

E

eagle, eagles, eaglet

eagle eye (n.), **eagle-eyed** (adj.)

Eagle Scout Capitalize this rank of the Boy Scouts of America.

Eakins, Thomas (1844–1916) American painter.

earth Lowercase generally; capitalize *Earth* when used as the proper name of the planet, for example, with reference to other planets: Mars is the planet closest to *Earth*.

Earth Day

Earth First! The exclamation point is part of the name, so it is best to avoid ending a sentence with this term.

earthquake Lowercase when referring to particular earthquakes: *the San Francisco earthquake of 1906.*

earthworm

easement a right-of-way over land you do not own.

east, eastern Always lowercase when *east* and *eastern* are used as directions or simple descriptive terms: The sun rises in the *east*. A book on *eastern* wildflowers. Also lowercase when part of the common name of a plant or animal.

Capitalize when *east* is used as part of the name of a region (whether actual or a state of mind): *the East, the East Coast.*

Whether to capitalize *east* in the expression *back east* depends on personal preference and context. It may be capitalized when referring to a specific destination: She went *back East* for her college reunion. It may be lowercase when the reference seems more general (as when people on the West Coast refer to, say, Cleveland as "back east"): "They don't have anything like this *back east*." Of course, if the term occurs several times in a text, it is less obtrusive to choose one spelling or the other and stick with it. See further discussion at **west**.

East Coast

easternmost

Eastern Shore Capitalize when referring to the Chesapeake Bay area.

Eastern standard time (EST), Eastern daylight time (EDT)

eastward not *eastwards.*

eco- Compounds with this prefix are written as one word: *ecosystem, ecotourism.*

Eco-Challenge the adventure race.

ecology/environment The field of study is *ecology; environment* refers to surroundings.

ecosystem Usually lowercase; however, may be capitalized in a phrase such as *the Greater Yellowstone Ecosystem,* if done consistently. This is most appropriate in a text about that area.

Eden in the Bible and as a general term.

eelgrass

e.g. *for example* preferred. If *e.g.* is used, set off with commas, and do not italicize.

EIS, environmental impact statement

elbowroom (n.)

Elderhostel a nonprofit organization offering travel and educational programs for people age fifty-five and older.

elevations use *feet*, not ' or *ft.* Exception: The symbol or abbreviation may be used in maps, rock climbing guides, and field guides. Use numerals: *7,709-foot* East Temple at Zion National Park. Durango is set at an elevation of *6,512 feet.*

The term *elevation* is more likely to be used when giving a measurement. The term *altitude* tends to appear in more general contexts: *high altitude, altitude sickness.*

elk (sing., pl.), **bull, cow, calf**

El Niño

e-mail

embark Also see **debark/disembark.**

emigrant, emigrate To *emigrate* is to leave a country or region; to *immigrate* is to enter or settle in a new country. The people who settled the American West were *emigrants* from one region of the United States to another region, not *immigrants.* Note the name, *the Emigrant Wilderness,* in California.

EMT, emergency medical technician

en route (adv., adj.)

endangered species a species in danger of becoming extinct throughout all or a portion of its range. The federal government maintains a list of threatened and endangered species. These designations are lowercase.

Some species are listed as threatened or endangered by a state but not by the federal government or vice versa. Use the terms "state-listed endangered," "state-listed threatened," "federally listed threatened," or "federally listed endangered" to describe the status of specific species. Note: there is no hyphen in *federally listed.*

Avoid the ambiguous constructions "federally endangered" or "state threatened."

Species of special concern is an official designation for a species to which wildlife experts devote special attention because it is rare, especially disturbed by people, or necessary for the survival of other species.

The terms *rare* and *common* may be used in a general sense; that is, a species that is not officially endangered or threatened may still be described as *rare.* If *rare* is used often in a text, the author may wish to define the limits of the term.

Endangered Species Act (1973)

endo

enervate, enervating means "to weaken"; the opposite of *energize.*

Engelmann spruce not *Englemann spruce.*

enormity (n.)/**enormous** (adj.) Use *enormity* to refer to something that is morally terrible, *enormous* to refer to something very large. Do not refer to the *enormity* of a canyon. *Enormity* is not the noun form of *enormous.*

Ensolite a trademark.

ensure/insure To *ensure* is to make sure; to *insure* is to protect with insurance.

environment See usage note at **ecology.**

Environment Canada a Canadian government department.

Environmental Protection Agency, EPA

equator, equatorial lowercase.

equinox lowercase. Spring and fall or vernal and autumnal equinoxes; summer and winter **solstices.**

era a division of geologic time comprising one or more periods. Lowercase. The three *eras* generally recognized are the Paleozoic, Mesozoic, and Cenozoic.

ergonomic (adj.)

ermine (sing., pl.)

escarpment Lowercase as a term descriptive of a kind of **formation,** a cliff formed when two more or less level areas are separated by erosion or faulting: *the Notch Peak escarpment.*

esker a serpentine ridge of gravel or sand deposited by a stream that once ran within a decaying glacier.

Eskimo, Eskimos It is preferable to specify the Eskimo people: *Inupiaq Eskimo,* or simply *Inupiaq,* for example. Use the preferred spelling of the particular people being discussed.

Eskimo roll also known simply as a *roll.*

espresso a camp *espresso* maker, not *expresso.*

estivate (v.) to spend the summer especially dormant; the term corresponding to hibernate. The noun is *estivation.*

estrus (n.)/**estrous** (adj.) *Estrus* is the time when a female mammal is in heat.

estuary where a river meets the tides of a sea.

estufa the old Spanish word for **kiva.** Use only when citing historical references.

ethnicity In general, try to use the name preferred by the group in question. See entries for **Indian, Hispanic, African American,** etc.

etriers also called **aiders.**

Everglades, Florida Everglades the swampy area that includes Everglades National Park. Lowercase, *everglade* refers to a tract of swampy land covered mostly with tall grass.

ever-present (adj.)

every day (adv.), **everyday** (adj.) They try to go hiking *every day.* For them, hiking is an *everyday* occurrence.

exhausting/exhaustive *Exhausting* means tiring: an *exhausting* hike. *Exhaustive* means thorough: an *exhaustive* guidebook to day hikes in Yellowstone National Park.

exit Lowercase, in directions, when used with the name of a street or other place: *Take the Orange Street exit.* Also lowercase when used with a number: *Take exit 14.*

expedition names Capitalize the name of a historically significant expedition or exploring party: *the Donner Party, the Hayden Survey, the Lewis and Clark Expedition.* Lowercase when referring to a contemporary group.

extra- Compounds with *extra* are written as one word when *extra* means "beyond": *extraterrestrial, extraterritorial.* When *extra* is used as an intensifier, hyphenate: *an extra-thick pair of socks.*

eye-catching (adj.), **eye-popping** (adj.)

F

face climbing

Fahrenheit In text, use the abbreviation *F* (no period) instead of the word *Fahrenheit: 57 degrees F.* To give a range of temperatures: *The temperature can drop 15 to 20 degrees after sundown.* To give negative temperatures: *-15 degrees F* or *15 below zero,* not *minus 15.*

In cookbooks, field guides, hot springs guides, and other books where space is at a premium and temperatures are noted throughout, use the degree symbol: *Bake at 375° for 3 hours.* Fahrenheit temperatures are assumed in such cases.

faint/feint You may feel dizzy and *faint* at high altitude. A *feint* is a deception.

fair Capitalize when part of a proper name: *the Western Montana Fair, the Crow Fair,* but *the fair.*

Falcon a registered trademark of Falcon Publishing, Inc. Acceptable second reference; first reference should be to Falcon Publishing. No longer *Falcon Press.*

FalconGuides a series of recreational guidebooks produced by Falcon. A registered trademark of Falcon.

fall line

falls a waterfall; can take a singular or a plural verb. Capitalize when commonly considered part of the proper name: *Hidden Falls, the falls.* Lowercase when *falls* is used descriptively, as for unnamed waterfalls: *the Blodgett Creek falls.*

If a waterfall has an upper and a lower part, capitalize the short forms of those names: *the Upper Falls and Lower Falls of the Grand Canyon of the Yellowstone.* Note: This is consistent with the guideline for **river names.**

false cast

fanny pack

faraway (adj.)

far-flung (adj.)

Farmer John, Farmer Jane Capitalize the names of these styles of wetsuits.

farmhouse but **ranch house**

farmland

far-ranging

farther/further Use *farther* for physical distance: "Go a little *farther* down the trail." Use *further* to express time or degree: "We need to discuss this *further*."

Far West the region of the United States.

fast food (n.), **fast-food** (adj.) as in *a fast-food restaurant*.

fat pine, fatwood

fault Capitalize the name of a fault: *the San Andreas Fault, the fault.*

faun/fawn A *faun* is a mythological creature; a *fawn* is a young deer.

fauna Like **flora**, a singular noun used as a collective. Takes a singular verb unless the context clearly calls for a plural, as in "The local fauna compete among themselves for food."

feat/feet A *feat* is a deed; not *feet*, the unit of distance or plural of "foot."

federal Lowercase generally: *federal*, state, and local governments. Capitalize only when part of the formal name of an agency or program, as in *Federal Duck Stamp Program* or *Federal Trade Commission.*

Federal Land Policy and Management Act of 1976 governs management of **BLM** lands.

fenceline (n.)

feral describes a wild representative of a domesticated species: *feral cat, feral pig.*

ferryboat

fetlock/forelock A *fetlock* is part of a horse's leg; a *forelock* is part of a horse's mane.

fiberglass generally, as in *a fiberglass paddle.* Use the spelling *Fiberglas* only when referring to the trademarked material.

-field Compounds with *field* are usually written as one word when the field produces some kind of resource: *coalfield, hayfield, oilfield.* Two words when the first word merely describes the field: *old fields, stubble fields.*

field-dress (v.), **field-dressed, field dressing**

field guide (n.)

field-test (v.), **field-tested, field test** (n.)

fieldwork (n.)

fifi hook used in aid climbing.

figure-8 belay device, figure-8 knot Use the numeral, as it indicates the shape better than does the spelled-out word.

figure skater, figure skating refers specifically to the skating of figures; use **ice skating** for the general term.

film 35mm *film*

fingerling a young fish, larger than a minnow.

-fire One word: *brushfire, wildfire.* Exception: *forest fire.*

fire- One word: *firearm, firefighter, firefly, fireproof, firewood, fireworks.* Two words: *fire ant, fire brigade, fire department, fire pan, fire ring, fire road, fire tower.*

firebreak one word

firn compacted old snow; an alternate term for **névé.**

first aid (n.), **first-aid** (adj.) *a first-aid kit.*

first come, first served no hyphens in this phrase.

firsthand (adj., adv.)

fish (generally), **fish** (pl. of one species), **fishes** (pl. of more than one species)

fish Compound verbs with *fish* are written as two words: *ice fishing, sport fishing.*

fish camp but **hunting camp.**

fisher the mammal.

fishhook *Hook* preferred. When stating the size of a hook: *a No.4 hook*, not *#4 hook*.

fishing rod not *fishing pole* unless referring to a kid with a stick. When stating the weight of a rod, use numerals: *a 7-weight rod.*

fish ladder

fixed anchor, fixed hardware, fixed rope

fjord not *fiord*, except in the brand of lures: *a Fiord Spoon.*

flag (v.), **flagging** in rock climbing, to extend a hand or a foot to counterbalance, to keep from **barn-dooring.**

flair/flare One may execute a backflip with *flair;* but *flares* are flashes of light.

flamingo, flamingos

flammable able to catch fire; but **inflammable** preferred.

flammulated owl

flapjack

flare a flame; see note at **flair.**

flash (v.) to climb a route with no falls, rests, or information about the route.

flash flood not *flashflood.*

flashlight

flat-foot (v.), **flat-footing** the crampon technique.

Flathead Indian usually refers to the Bitterroot Salish Indians, the Pend d'Oreille/Kalispel Indians, or the Kootenai Indians, who have all inhabited the Flathead Valley in western Montana. Use a specific tribe's name in all cases.

flatland(s)

flatlander

flatwater as in *flatwater canoeing.*

fleece/pile *Pile* is the way yarns are looped to produce *fleece,* a kind of fabric. *Fleece* can be either wool or synthetic, although it is generally used now to refer to synthetic fabrics such as **Polarfleece.**

flies and lures Capitalize every word of the names of specific fly patterns or lures; lowercase words that generally describe a series, type, or kind of fly or lure or the insect species they imitate: *Dark Cahill, Olive Woolly Worm, Elk Hair Caddis, Coachman, Royal Coachman,* but *streamers, dragonfly nymphs, terrestrials, caddis fly, midge, salmon fly.* When in doubt about whether insect names are one word or two *(mayfly, stonefly, caddis fly, salmon fly),* consult the *American Heritage Dictionary.*

Brand names of lures are always capitalized and spelled according to the manufacturer's style: *Dardevle, Need-L-Eel, Wob-L-Rite.* Lowercase generic terms like *jig, plug, spinner,* and *spoon* when used alone. Capitalize such terms when they appear as part of a brand name: *Tony Accetta Pet Spoon.*

floatplane or **seaplane;** *a floatplane service.*

floatation an incorrect spelling; use **flotation.**

floe as in an *ice floe;* not *flow.*

floodplain not *flood plain.*

flood stage

flood tide not *floodtide.*

floodwall

floodwater(s)

flora Like **fauna,** a singular noun used as a collective. Takes a singular verb unless the context clearly calls for a plural, as in "On this hike, you can see spectacular examples of desert flora, which bloom in March and April." In this sentence, the word *examples* highlights the individual plants that make up the collective flora.

Florida Keys

flotation not *floatation.*

flotation bag

flotation device

flotsam/jetsam Wreckage floating after a shipwreck is *flotsam;*

items intentionally thrown overboard, or jettisoned, are *jetsam.*

-flower Compounds ending in *flower* are usually written as one word: *sunflower.*

flower names See **plant names** and **taxonomy.**

fluorescence, fluorine, fluorite Note the spellings.

-fly Compound nouns with *fly* that are written as one word: *horsefly, mayfly.* Two words: *rain fly* (as on a tent). For other insect names, consult the *American Heritage Dictionary.*

flycaster not *fly-caster.*

fly-fish (v.)

fly fisher not *fly fisherman* or *fly fisherwoman.*

fly fishing (n.) not *fly-fishing.* Also *dry-fly fishing; wet-fly fishing; nymph fishing.*

fly line Use numerals when stating the weight of a line, from 1 to 15 (1 is the lightest): *a 4-weight fly line.* Hyphenate the compound adjectives in phrases such as *a double-taper line, a sink-tip line, a weight-forward line.*

fly-over (n.)

fly rod Use numerals when giving the length and weight of a rod: *an 8-foot rod, a 6-weight rod.*

fly tying, fly tier not *fly-tying, fly-tier.*

flyway a bird migration route. Capitalize the names of flyways: *Central Flyway, Pacific Flyway.*

fo'c's'le short for *forecastle;* common in a nautical context.

fog bank

foghorn

föhn a warm, dry wind that occurs in the Alps.

Folbot manufacturer of folding kayaks.

-fold Compounds that end in *fold* are written as one word: *twofold, hundredfold.*

folf Frisbee golf; *disc golf* preferred, because *Frisbee* is a trademark.

folk One word: *folklore, folkways.* One word preferred: *folktale.*

Two words: *folk art, folk medicine, folk music, folk remedy.* Two words preferred: *folk song, folk dance.* It is fine to have *folklore* and *folk song* in one text, as long as the spelling of individual words remains consistent.

Also: *countryfolk*

fool's gold

foot- Compound nouns beginning with *foot* are usually written as one word: *footbridge, foothill, footpath, footprint, footwear, footwork.* Exceptions: *foot brake, foot brace* (as in a kayak), *foot jam* (the climbing technique).

forb not a grass.

ford Capitalize when part of a proper name of a river or stream crossing: *Bechler Ford.*

forego/forgo To *forego* is to go before, more commonly seen in the forms *foregoing* and *foregone.* To *forgo* is to give up: *forgo a chance at the summit.*

foreign words Italicize only if they are not in common English usage. *"Au revoir!"* the French climber cried. No italics: "Their car broke down en route." A good guideline: if the word appears in the main portion of the dictionary, and not in a section of foreign words and phrases, then it need not be italicized.

foreset in geology, one layer of deposition of a delta, along with *bottomset* and *topset.* Not *forset.*

forest Capitalize when part of a proper name, whether a state or national forest or simply a traditional name, such as *Black Forest.*

forest ranger

Forest Service Use *USDA Forest Service,* not *U.S. Forest Service.* Forest Service is acceptable in subsequent references.

foreword/forward A *foreword* is an introductory note at the beginning of a book, usually written by someone other than the author. *Forward* is a direction.

fork If a fork of a river has its own name, as in *West Fork of* *the Flathead River,* capitalize short forms of the name in subsequent references: *West Fork.* The same guideline applies to branches: *East Branch Chandler River.*

formation Lowercase this word when referring to geologic formations: *Cutler formation, Morrison formation, Entrada sandstone, Mancos shale.*

Formica a trademark.

fort Capitalize when part of name: *Fort Kearny.* Spell out in text, but okay to abbreviate as *Ft.* on maps and charts and in captions.

foul-weather (adj.)

Four Corners area or region. The four states that meet are Arizona, Colorado, New Mexico, and Utah. Capitalize the *Four Corners Monument,* the name of the actual marker.

four-by-four vehicle preferred over *4x4 vehicle.*

4-H Club preferred over *Four-H.*

fourteeners 14,000-foot peaks, especially in Colorado.

four-way stop

four-wheel drive (n.), **four-wheel-drive** (adj.) as in *a four-wheel-drive vehicle.* Not *4WD vehicle.* The abbreviation *4WD* is acceptable as a road description on maps, but not in running text.

four-wheeler

Fourth of July

fox, foxes, dog fox, vixen, kit

Fred Harvey Company

free (v.) in rock climbing.

free climbing

free-flowing (adj.) as an undammed waterway.

free soloing

free-standing (adj.)

freestyle (adj., adv.)

freeze-dried (adj.)

Fremont prehistoric Indian culture of the southwest.

Frémont, John Charles (1813–1890) American soldier, politician, explorer. Write his last name with an accent, although the many places named after him do not retain the accent: *Fremont Peak*.

French and Indian Wars

French Canadian (n.) when referring to the ethnic group. Not *Canuck*, which is offensive. Hyphenate the adjective form: *French-Canadian* cuisine.

freshwater (adj.) except *Fresh Water* in the name of the Florida Commission. For the noun, two words when *fresh* modifies *water*; "*Fresh water* is available for drinking." One word when *freshwater* is a substance, in contrast to *salt water*; "They prefer *freshwater* for boating."

friable/fryable *Friable* means crumbly, used of soil; *fryable*, something that can be fried.

friction climbing

Friend trademark for a spring-loaded camming device made by Wild Country.

Frisbee

front Compounds with *front* are usually written as one word: *beachfront, lakefront, waterfront*. Capitalize *front* when part of the name of a mountain range: *the Front Range, the Wasatch Front*.

frontcountry a National Park Service term referring to areas in national parks that are accessible to vehicles. The **backcountry** is defined as any area not accessible to vehicles. Use the term *frontcountry* only when referring specifically to a national park or to National Park Service literature.

front-point, front-pointing a crampon technique. But: "Check the *front points* of your crampons."

Front Range part of the Rockies in Colorado.

frostbite, frostbitten

frost heave

frost line the maximum depth to which the ground becomes frozen.

fry bread (n.)

full- Compound adjectives that begin with *full* are hyphenated before the noun: *a full-time job.* After the noun, no need to hyphenate: *He works full time as a guide.*

fumarole not *fumerole.*

fungus Use the plural form **fungi**, not *funguses.*

further/farther See note at **farther.**

G

gabbro

Gadsden Purchase

gaiters the covering for the ankles or the neck; not *gators*, short for alligators.

Gambel oak not *gambrel*.

Gambel's quail

gamble/gambol To *gamble* is to take a chance or make a bet; to *gambol* is to frolic.

game fish (n.) or **gamefish** author preference, but be consistent.

game trail the narrow trail made by elk, deer, or other game.

gamy (adj.) preferred over *gamey*.

gang capitalize the name of a gang of outlaws: *James Brothers*.

garter snake

gas The preferred form for the plural is **gases,** not *gasses*.

Gatorade

gators not *'gators;* short for *alligators;* okay in informal contexts, as in quoted speech.

gauge not *gage*. The size of shotguns is stated as gauge, not caliber: *a 10-gauge shotgun, a 12-gauge shotgun*. Note the decimal in *a .410-gauge shotgun*. Also see **guns.** Also: *narrow-gauge railroad*.

gazetteer

gear sling

Geiger counter

Gemini cord

gemstone

General Allotment Act See **Dawes Act.**

genus and species names Capitalize the first word (genus) and lowercase the second (species): *Castor canadensis* (beaver). Both words are italicized. For further discussion, see **taxonomy**.

geo- Compounds beginning with *geo* are written as one word: *geomagnetic, geophysical*.

geoduck a clam found on the coast of the Pacific Northwest. Not **gweduc**.

geologic, geological Usage may sometimes be a matter of how it sounds. Generally, use *geologic* in phrases such as *a geologic era, geologic time.* Use *geological* when referring to the study of geology: *geological survey, a geological field trip.* Compare **historic, historical**.

geologic eras In names of geologic eras—*the Precambrian era, the Cretaceous period, the Pleistocene epoch*—capitalize the first word and lowercase the second, generic term.

geological survey See **U.S. Geological Survey**.

ger a kind of Mongolian tent.

Geronimo (1829?–1909) the Apache leader.

getaway (n.)

geyser Capitalize their names: *Old Faithful, Oblong Geyser, Sentinel Cone.*

Ghost Dance Capitalize, as the name of a cultural movement. Note: lowercase *sun dance*, the name of a dance.

ghost town

Giardia lamblia the bacteria that causes the disease **giardiasis**. Capitalize and italicize following rules for taxonomy. *Giardia* okay on second reference.

giardiasis a nasty intestinal disorder caused by bacteria often found in streams.

giftbook

Gila monster

Gilpin, Laura (1891–1979) photographer known for work in the Southwest.

Girl Scouts of the United States of America *Girl Scouts* on
second reference. Also see **Boy Scouts of America.**

girth-hitch (v.)

glacial lake Capitalize in names of ancient lakes: *Glacial
Lake Missoula.*

glissade (v.) a sliding step used on snow or ice.

global positioning system, GPS

Going-to-the-Sun Road in Glacier National Park.

gold coast There is more than one of these in the world. The
term may be capitalized, but should be consistent within a
text. Also see **place names.**

gold country Lowercase, as in *the California gold country.*

goldfield(s)

gold rush Lowercase, as a descriptive term: *the California gold
rush, the Alaska gold rush.*

golden eagle

Golden Eagle Passport or **Golden Eagle pass.** The annual
national parks pass. The other kinds of national parks passes
are the **Golden Age Passport** (lifetime entry for those age 62
and older) and the **Golden Access Passport** (free lifetime
entry for those who are blind or permanently disabled).

golden trout *golden(s)* on second reference.

goose, geese, gander, goose, gosling

goose down (n.)

gooseneck (n.) appears as part of some place names: *the
Goosenecks of the San Juan River; the Goosenecks Overlook* (Capitol
Reef National Park). Lowercase if used merely descriptively.
Consult a USGS map or the land management agency.

gopher the small mammal; not *gofer,* someone who runs errands.

Gore-Tex a trademark of W. L. Gore & Associates, Inc.

gorp another term for *trail mix.* In all caps, GORP is an
acronym for Great Outdoor Recreation Pages, an outdoors website.

government departments *Bureau of Indian Affairs; the bureau* or

BIA on second reference. *Department of the Interior, the Interior Department, the department.* For state government departments, use an ampersand or the word "and," depending on the preference of that department: *Montana Department of Fish, Wildlife & Parks.* On second reference, *Montana Fish, Wildlife & Parks* is acceptable.

Capitalize the full, formal names of government programs: *the Wild and Scenic Rivers System.* See appendixes for names of government departments and agencies.

GPS, global positioning system

grade Capitalize when part of a road name: *Laureles Grade.*

graffiti (pl.) usually takes a singular verb: *Graffiti is a problem at this rock art site.*

granary not *grainary.*

Grand Canyon of the Yellowstone or *Yellowstone Canyon, the canyon.* The short form *Grand Canyon* is acceptable if it is clear that Yellowstone is meant (and not Grand Canyon National Park).

Grand Coulee

Grand Staircase–Escalante National Monument managed by the Bureau of Land Management, not the National Park Service. Capitalize the term *Grand Staircase* when used alone.

grand tour (n.)

granny gear

grapevine

-grass One word: *cheatgrass, tallgrass.* Two words: *bunch grass.*

grassland(s)

grassroots (pl. n., adj.)

graupel snow pellets.

gray not *grey,* when referring generally to the color; but *greyhound; Greyhound Lines, Inc.; Two Grey Hills,* New Mexico (and a style of Navajo rug); and *Zane Grey.* The fly pattern is *Gray Wulff.* Follow USGS for spelling of landforms: *Gray,* peaks in the Adirondacks and Yellowstone National Park; *Greylock,* peaks in Massachusetts and Colorado.

Great American Desert Capitalize in historical references to
   the West.
Great Basin
greater capitalize when used with an urban area: *Greater Austin.*
   Lowercase the word "area" if it follows: *the Greater Austin area.*
great house a large Anasazi dwelling. May be capitalized,
   depending on author preference.
Great Lakes Lake Erie, Lake Huron, Lake Michigan, Lake
   Ontario, and Lake Superior. Lowercase if referring to them
   on second reference as *the lakes.*
Great Lakes states usually considered Minnesota, Wisconsin,
   and Michigan, although Illinois, Indiana, Ohio, Pennsylvania,
   and New York all have Great Lakes shoreline.
Great Northern Railway
Great Plains or **the Plains** The Great Plains region is roughly
   defined as extending from North Dakota to Texas and from
   the Rocky Mountains to the Missouri River.
   Lowercase a directional word that precedes *Plains: northern
   Great Plains, southwestern Plains.*
Greeley, Horace (1811–1872) journalist, editor of the *New
   York Tribune,* who said "Go west, young man."
green capitalize *Green* when referring to the political party or
   movement. Lowercase when referring generally to environ-
   mentally sound products or practices.
greenbelt
greenhouse effect
Green Tortoise bus line run by Green Tortoise Adventure Travel.
Greenwich mean time (GMT)
grey Use the spelling *gray,* unless it is *grey* in a proper name.
   See examples at **gray.**
Grey, Zane (1875–1939) author of many Western novels.
Grigri belay device made by Petzl.
grill/grille a *grill* is for cooking; a *grille* is a decorative grate, as
   on the front of a car.

grisly means "gruesome." The camper suffered a *grisly* attack by the *grizzly* bear.

grizzly bear *(Ursus arctos)* a subspecies of brown bear; *grizzly bears* preferred for plural, but *grizzlies* acceptable. The Alaskan brown bear is also a subspecies, *Ursus arctos middendorffi*. Kodiak bears are Alaskan brown bears on Kodiak Island.

grotto, grottoes preferred over *grottos* for plural.

groundhog or **woodchuck** Both are terms for **marmots.** *Groundhog Day* is February 2.

ground squirrel, ground squirrels

ground water, groundwater author's preference, but be consistent.

grouse (sing., pl.), **chick**

guanaco, guanacos a South American mammal.

guardrail

Guatemala not *Guatamala*.

guesthouse

guest room

guidebook

guillemet/guillemot A *guillemet* is a French quotation mark; a *guillemot* is a bird, a kind of auk.

Guinness Book of World Records

gulch Capitalize when part of a proper name: *Grand Gulch,* but *the gulch.*

Gulf Coast Capitalize when referring to the region, *the Gulf Coast.* The Gulf Coast states are those along the Gulf of Mexico: Texas, Louisiana, Mississippi, Alabama, and Florida. Lowercase when referring to the actual shoreline: beaches along the *Gulf coast.*

Gulf Intracoastal Waterway *Intracoastal Waterway* okay on first reference.

Gulf of Mexico Also capitalize *the Gulf* on second reference, an exception to the usual rule for terms that stand alone.

Gulf Stream *the stream* on second reference.

gumbo In outdoor contexts, *gumbo* usually refers to silty soil
   that forms a sticky mud when wet (not the Cajun stew).

guns Capitalize brand names such as *Colt, Remington, Winchester,*
   and *Smith & Wesson* (the ampersand is okay).

   Caliber: diameter of the inside of a gun barrel, stated in
   millimeters or decimal fractions of an inch: *a 9 mm pistol, a
   .22-caliber rifle, a .38-caliber pistol, a .45-caliber revolver.*

   Gauge: number per pound of lead balls that have the same
   diameter as the gun barrel: *a 10-gauge shotgun, a 12-gauge
   shotgun.* Exception: a decimal is used in *a .410-gauge shotgun.*

   The word *Magnum* is capitalized: *a .44-caliber Magnum.*

   Shells contain shot (buckshot is large-size shot). Cartridges
   contain bullets.

   Distinctions between guns: A rifle has a rifled bore (spiral
   grooves in the barrel). A shotgun has a smooth bore; it is a
   smoothbore gun. A shotgun may be *double-barreled.*

gunwale not *gunnel.*

gutpile one word to describe what a scavenging animal may
   feed on.

gweduc Use **geoduck,** the preferred spelling.

H

hailstone

hailstorm

half- Compounds that are hyphenated: *half-hour, half-light, half-moon*. Compounds that are not hyphenated: *halftone* (the printing process), *halfway*.

Half Dome

half-hour or **half an hour** never *a half an hour*.

halfpipe one word in a snowboarding context.

Halley's comet The word *comet* is lowercase.

hall of fame, halls of fame Capitalize when part of a proper name: *the Cowgirl Hall of Fame, the hall of fame*.

hammerhead

hammock a hanging seat; in the southern United States, also another word for a *hummock*, a forested knoll in a marshy area. Follow local usage.

handbook

handhold

handicapped Do not use. See entry at **disability**.

hand jam (n., v.), **hand jamming** not *hand-jam, hand-jamming*.

handlebars

handmade (adj.)

hands-on (adj.)

hangdogging resting during a climb. Not *hang-dogging*.

hang glider (n.), **hang glide** (v.), **hang gliding** (n.)

hantavirus not the *Navajo flu.*

hardpan a road surface; also known as **caliche.**

hardwood

hare, hares, leverets

Harpers Ferry not *Harper's Ferry.*

Harte, Bret (1836–1902) author of Western tales. *Brett* was his given middle name, but *Bret* was his pen name.

haul bag in big-wall climbing, used to haul gear up a cliff.

haul-out (n.), **haul out** (v.) place where a seal or sea lion comes ashore: "You can observe sea lions at a favorite *haul-out.*"

haversack

Hawaii (n.), Hawaiian (adj.) The eight major Hawaiian Islands are (from largest to smallest) Hawai'i, Maui, O'ahu, Kaua'i, Moloka'i, Lana'i, Ni'ihau, and Kaho'olawe. The backward apostrophe represents a glottal stop. If used in a text, should be used consistently throughout.

Hawaii standard time Daylight-saving time is not observed in Hawaii.

hawk, hawks, eyas

HawkWatch a nonprofit organization that works to protect raptors.

hawthorn a species of thorny tree or shrub; not *Hawthorne,* the nineteenth-century American novelist.

hay fever

haystack

hay wagon

Hayden, Ferdinand V. (1829–1887) led U.S. Geological Survey expeditions to Yellowstone.

HB (Hugh Banner) a brand of wedge or nut.

head lamp/headlamp People wear *head lamps;* cars have *headlamps* (but *headlights* preferred when referring to cars).

headland(s) Follow local usage in capitalizing: *the Marin Headlands,* in local usage and usage of the Golden Gate

National Recreation Area. *Headlands* takes a plural verb, even when referring to an area as a unit.

headwall the slope or cliff at the head of a valley or cirque.

headwaters (n.) takes a singular verb, as the meaning, the source of a river, is singular.

headwind

heat Compounds with *heat* are usually written as two words: *heat exhaustion, heat lightning, heat rash, heat stroke, heat wave.*

heel hook the climbing move.

Heimlich maneuver

heli-skiing, helicopter skiing

hellgrammite dobsonfly larva.

Hells Canyon no apostrophe.

hemisphere Capitalize when naming a specific region: the *Western Hemisphere,* but *the hemisphere.*

Henie, Sonja (1912–1969) ice skater.

herbaceous

heronry

Hexentric a brand name of Black Diamond. Not *Hexcentric.* The short form *hexes* usually appears lowercase, and is often used generically to describe the same shape of nut made by other manufacturers.

hibachi

hideaway (n.)

hideout (n.)

high country (n.), **high-country** (adj.)

High Country News no hyphen.

high tide

Hi-Line not *High Line.* The stretch of northern Montana along the route of the Great Northern Railway.

highway Capitalize when part of the name of a road: *the Beartooth Highway, the highway.* Also see **Maps, Roads, and Directions, p. 14.**

hillside

hilltop

hinterland

Hispanic Use with caution. More specific ethnic terms are preferred: **Puerto Rican, Mexican American.**

historic/historical A *historic* place or event is of great significance: The Battle of the Little Bighorn was a *historic* occasion. *Historical* applies more generally to monuments, agencies, and other things that commemorate the past: a *historical* society, a *historical* novel.

In the names of units of the National Park System, it is almost always *historic* in names of sites: *Manzanar National Historic Site.* It is almost always *historical* in names of parks: *Chaco Culture National Historical Park.* See **Appendix A: National Parks, Monuments, etc.**

Never precede either word with the article *an.*

hitchhike (v.), **hitchhiker** (n.)

hoard/horde A *hoard* is an accumulation of something: *a hoard of gold.* A *horde* is a large group—of people, or of wasps or hornets.

hogan a traditional Navajo house.

hogback, hogback ridge

Hohokam a prehistoric American Indian culture of Arizona.

hold One word: *foothold, handhold, toehold.*

hole a deep part of a river.

Hole-in-the-Rock Trail

holidays Capitalize the names of holidays: "The park is closed on *Christmas Day* and *New Year's Day.*" Note the position of the apostrophes in *April Fools' Day, Mother's Day, Presidents' Day.* Capitalize: *Fourth of July, the Fourth.* Also capitalize designations of days, weeks, and months: *Earth Day, Native American Heritage Month.* Lowercase the word *weekend: Labor Day weekend.*

holistic not *wholistic* (a common misspelling).

Hollofil trademark for a kind of insulation.

home If a home is considered a destination for visitors and is managed as such, capitalize: *the Mary Austin Home, the Wolfe Cabin* (at Arches National Park). Do not capitalize if the term *home, cabin, farm,* etc. is simply descriptive: "Stop by the fruit stand at the *Smith farm.*" Also see **building**.

Homestead Act (1862)

Homo sapiens the human species. As a scientific name, the first word is capitalized; however, the term need not be italicized in a general context.

hoodoo(s) free-standing pillars of stone developed by erosion, most often found in the desert Southwest.

hoof, hoofs or **hooves** author preference for plural, but be consistent.

hook preferred over *fishhook.* When stating size: *a No. 4 hook,* not *#4 hook.* Alternatively: *a size 4 hook* (but style should be consistent throughout text).

hookup (n.) a campground with RV *hookups.*

Hopewell the prehistoric Indian culture centered in what is now Ohio.

horde See note at **hoard**.

hornblende

horno Spanish for "oven." The outdoor ovens found in the Southwest. Not italicized.

horns are permanent; **antlers** are periodically shed and regrown.

horse, horses, stallion (**gelding** if neutered), **mare, foal** (**filly** if female, **colt** if male)

horseback You go *horseback riding,* or *ride on horseback,* or *ride horseback.* Not *ride ahorseback* except in informal usage, as in quoted speech.

horsefly

horsepacking traveling on horseback and camping for one or more nights.

horseshoe

hostel

hot-air balloon

hotshot (n.)

hot spot (n.)

hot spring(s) Capitalize when part of a proper name: *Burgdorf Hot Springs, the hot springs.*

hot tub

hour The hike took *two hours;* it was a *two-hour* hike.

house *farmhouse,* but *ranch house, row house.*

House of Refuge in historical references. *Houses of Refuge* sheltered stranded sailors. They were run by the U.S. Life Saving Service.

Hovercraft a trademark, so should be capitalized. Generic term: an *air-cushion vehicle.*

how-to (adj.) a *how-to* book.

Hudson River school

Hudson's Bay Company The place is *Hudson Bay.*

hueco in rock climbing, a pocket hold; named after *Hueco Tanks* in Texas. Do not italicize.

Huffman, L. A. (1854–1931) photographer who worked mainly in Montana.

humans, humanity preferred to *man.*

humpback whale not *humpbacked whale.*

hunter-gatherer (n.)

hunting camp but **fish camp.**

hurricane names are capitalized and set in roman type: *Hurricane Andrew.*

hut-to-hut skiing

hydration pack generic term for the CamelBak type of water container.

hydroelectric no hyphen.

Hypalon a synthetic rubber used, for example, in rafts.

hyper- The prefix *hyper* means "over." Compounds are written as one word: *hyperextend, hyperthermia, hyperthermic, hyperventilate.*

hyphenation See **Compounds and Hyphenation,** p. 5, and individual entries.

hypo- The prefix *hypo* means "below." Compounds are written as one word: *hypothermia, hypothermic.*

hypoxia (n.) a lack of oxygen.

I

ice Two words: *ice chest, ice cream, ice floe, ice fog, ice pack, ice storm, ice water.* One word: *iceberg, iceboat, icebreaker, icecap, icefall.*

ice age When used alone, typically refers to the most recent ice age; do not capitalize. Capitalize only the proper nouns in the names of specific ice ages: *the Wisconsin ice age.*

ice ax (n.) or **ice axe,** depending on author preference, but be consistent.

ice climbing

ice-cold (adj.)

ice field, icefield Either is acceptable; just be consistent. Note that place names that include this term are usually written as one word: *the Columbia Icefield.*

ice fishing

ice screw protection for ice climbing; *an ice-screw placement.*

ice skate (n.), **ice skater** (n.), **ice-skate** (v.) Use *figure skating* only when referring specifically to the skating of figures.

Iditarod the dogsled race; follows the Iditarod National Historic Trail. The formal name is the *Iditarod Trail Sled Dog Race.* The *Iditasport* is a race for people (without dogs).

i.e. abbreviation for *id est,* Latin for "that is." Set off with commas.

igloo, igloos

IMAX

immigrant *Immigrants* to the United States come from another country; *emigrants* settled the American West by emigrating from one part of the country to another.

impairment the loss or abnormality of an organ or body mechanism, which may result in **disability.**

impassable/impassible/impassive *Impassable* means that passage is impossible: The road may be *impassable* when wet. *Impassible,* like *impassive,* refers to an inability to be emotionally affected.

impatiens the plant.

inch Hyphenate measurements before a noun: *1-inch webbing.* Note that millimeter measurements do not take a hyphen: *a 35 mm camera, a 9 mm pistol.*

incredible/incredulous *Incredible* means "unbelievable" or "amazing"; *incredulous* means "skeptical."

incut (n.)

Indian Use of specific tribal name is preferred. *Indian, American Indian,* and *Native American* are all acceptable, based on preference of tribe. Use the tribe's preferred spelling of its proper name. See **Appendix B: Indian tribes.**
Spelling and hyphenation of personal names should be handled on a case-by-case basis.

Indian summer

Indian Territory in the nineteenth century, land set aside for Indians.

Indian wars but capitalize the names of individual wars: *the Black Hawk War.*

indoor (adj.), **indoors** (adv.) The same rule applies for **outdoor, outdoors.**

inflammable (adj.) able to catch fire; preferred over **flammable.**

inflatable (adj., n.) as a noun, can refer to an inflatable raft or kayak.

in-flight (adj.)

inholding (n.)

initials word space in between, just as if the initials were spelled out as full names: *L. L. Bean.*

in-line skate (n.), **in-line skating, in-line skater** generic terms for the trademark *Rollerblade,* which must be capitalized.

in-line spinner lowercase; a kind of lure.

inner tube (n.) An *inner-tuber* is a person who floats in an *inner tube.*

innkeeper

inroad

ins and outs

inshore (adj., adv.)

inside out

Inside Passage the waterway from Puget Sound to Skagway.

insole or **innersole** author preference; either is acceptable.

instream (adj.)

insure/ensure To *insure* is to protect with insurance; to *ensure* is to make sure.

inter- as a prefix, means "between." Compounds are written as one word: *interstate, interurban.* Exception: *inter-tribal* in the names of some Indian events, as in the Gallup, New Mexico, *Inter-Tribal Indian Ceremonial.*

interagency (adj.)

International Biosphere Reserve, World Biosphere Reserve The correct designation is simply **Biosphere Reserve.** It is a designation of UNESCO's Man and the Biosphere Program. In the United States, a number of national parks have been designated Biosphere Reserves.

international date line the imaginary line along the 180th meridian.

Internet Form for Internet addresses: www.nps.gov/parks.html. Use all lowercase letters, roman type. Use a final period when the address falls at the end of a sentence.

interpretive preferred over *interpretative:* an *interpretive* center.

interstate See **Maps, Roads, and Directions,** p. 14.

intertidal (adj.)

interval/intervale An *interval* is an amount of space or time.

An *intervale*, in New England, is low-lying land along a river (elsewhere called *bottomland*).

Intracoastal Waterway On second reference, *the waterway*. Not *Intercoastal Waterway*, and not *intercostal*, which means "between the ribs."

Ironman one word for the triathlon in Hawaii.

irregardless a double negative. Use **regardless**.

Ishi (1860?–1916) the last Yahi Indian in California.

island(s) Capitalize when part of a proper name: the *San Juan Islands*, but *the islands* on second reference. Lowercase when *island* is written before the name: *the island of Antigua*.

island-hop (v.)

issei, issei a first-generation Japanese immigrant to the United States. **Nisei** are second-generation Japanese Americans, the children of *issei*. Lowercase, roman type.

Isthmus of Panama *the isthmus* on second reference.

J

jacal wattle-and-daub construction.

jackalope a legendary creature—half jackrabbit, half antelope—whose habitat is humorous postcards in the West.

jack-in-the-pulpit, jack-in-the-pulpits

jackknife

jack pine

jackrabbit

Jackson, William Henry (1843–1942) Western photographer.

Jackson Hole began as *Jackson's Hole*; original name may appear in historical references.

Jacuzzi a trademark; *hot tub* or *whirlpool spa*, generally.

jaeger a sea bird.

jaguarundi

jalapeño

jam (v.), **jamming** no hyphen in compound nouns: *hand jam*.

jam crack (n.)

James Brothers Capitalize the name of a gang of outlaws.

jammers the long, red, open-topped touring cars in Glacier National Park.

Japanese American (n.), **Japanese-American** (adj.) Also see **issei, nisei,** and **ethnicity.**

javelina, javelinas See **collared peccary.**

J-bar

Jeep, jeep Do not capitalize unless referring specifically to the brand of vehicle. Lowercase when referring to the military vehicle and in phrases like **jeep trail.**

jeep road, jeep trail a road or trail (usually **doubletrack**) traversable only by four-wheel-drive vehicle, or by horse, by mountain bike, or on foot.

jellyfish (sing., pl.) *jellyfishes* if referring to more than one species.

jerry-built/jury-rig See note at **jury-rig.**

jet boat

jet lag not *jetlag.*

jetsam, flotsam Things thrown overboard (jettisoned) are *jetsam;* wreckage floating after a shipwreck is *flotsam.*

Jet Ski a trademark, so must be capitalized.

jet stream

jetty Lowercase, as a descriptive term, when paired with the name of a body of water.

jimsonweed or **sacred datura**

jodhpur(s)

johnboat not *jonboat* or *jon boat.*

Joshua tree not *Joshua-tree.*

Joshua Tree National Park no longer Joshua Tree National Monument.

J stroke

judgment not *judgement.*

jug, jug hold (n.)

jug (v.), **jugging** ascending a rope, or *jumaring,* derived from **Jumar,** a brand of ascender.

Jumar (n.) a trademark; *ascender* or *mechanical ascender,* generally.

junco, juncos

junction Capitalize when part of a proper noun: *Glen Creek Junction,* but *the junction of Interstate 90 and Interstate 15.*

Juneau the capital of Alaska; not *Juno,* the Roman goddess.

jury-rig (v.) to improvise in an emergency (not *jerry-rig*): "They *jury-rigged* a raft to get across the river." The term *jerry-built* means something cheaply built, and should be avoided.

K

K2 the peak in the Karakoram Range. Also the name of a ski manufacturer.

kachina

Kalispel the Indian tribe; *Kalispell*, the town in Montana.

kame a conical hill or mound.

Kampgrounds of America, KOA

Karakoram Range

Kastmaster a brand of lures.

Katahdin, Mount the northern end of the Appalachian Trail.

kayak (n.), **sea kayak, river kayak**

kayak (v.), **kayaker** (n.), **sea kayaker** (n.)

Kearny, Kearney Note the spellings: *Fort Phil Kearny* (Wyoming); *Stephen W. Kearny; Kearny County* (Kansas); *Kearny,* a town in Wyoming; *Fort Kearny State Park* (Nebraska); but *Kearney,* a city and a county in Nebraska.

keelboat

Keet Seel cliff dwelling at Navajo National Monument. Not *Kiet Seel.*

kelly hump in mountain biking, a mound of dirt intended to block vehicle access on a road or trail.

Kern, Edward (1823–1863) artist and mapmaker who traveled with Frémont; the Kern River is named after him. His brother **Richard Kern** (1821–1853) was also an artist.

kernmantle rope not *kernmantel.*

kettle pond, kettle lake

Kevlar a trademark.

key a low island, as in the *Florida Keys.* Also spelled **cay.** Not **quay,** a wharf.

key ring

Kilauea active volcanic crater on the island of Hawaii.

kill in a river name, means "stream": thus *the Schuylkill,* not the *Schuylkill River,* which is redundant. Can also be a separate word: *Basher Kill* (New York).

kind, type may be used interchangeably. Use *species,* however, when the context calls for a precise, scientific term. Thus, in a hiking guidebook, "you may see several *kinds* of hawk" or "you may see several *types* of hawk"—either is appropriate. In a field guide or wildlife viewing guide: "This marsh is habitat for many bird *species.*"

King, Clarence (1842–1901) surveyed the 40th parallel; first director of the U.S. Geological Survey.

kinnikinnick not *kinnikinnic* or *kinnikinnik;* a Native American tobacco preparation; also a plant. May be spelled differently in proper names.

kiva not *estufa,* the Spanish term sometimes found in historical references.

Kleenex a trademark; *facial tissue(s),* generally.

Klemheist knot a friction knot.

klister ski wax. The term is from the Norwegian. Lowercase, roman type.

Kmart The "m" is lowercase. No hyphen.

knapsack

kneecap

knee-deep (adj.)

knifeblade a kind of piton.

knife-edge (n.)

knot a speed of 1 nautical mile per hour. A boat might travel at *5 knots,* but *5 knots per hour* is redundant.

knots, in climbing Usually write as separate words: *clove hitch,* *overhand loop, slip knot, square knot. Bowline* is one word. If the word *double* is part of the knot, do not hyphenate: *double bowline, double fisherman's knot.* Use a numeral in *figure-8 knot.*

Kodachrome

Kodak

kokanee salmon

kokopelli image of insectlike, humpbacked flute player that often appears in rock art of the Southwest.

Kootenai for the Indian tribe. The spelling of place names in Montana and Idaho is usually *Kootenai.* The spelling of Canadian place names varies; often *Kutenai, Kutenay,* or *Kootenay,* as in *Kootenay National Park.*

Korean American (n.), **Korean-American** (adj.) Also see **ethnicity.**

K ration no hyphen.

krummholz form of stunted trees, such as grow near **timberline.**

Kryptonite a brand of U-locks.

kudzu

L

Labrador retriever

laccolith

-lace Compounds with *lace* are generally written as one word: *bootlace, necklace, shoelace.*

ladyfish (n.)

lady's slipper

laguna *lake* in Spanish. Avoid redundancies in names.

lake Capitalize when part of a proper name: *Lake Tahoe, Flathead Lake,* but *the lake* on second reference. *Lake of the Woods, Great Salt Lake, Lake District* (England).
If a lake has several parts, each with its own name, capitalize short forms of the names on second reference: *Upper Waterton Lake, Middle Waterton Lake, Lower Waterton Lake; the Upper Lake.* Note: This is consistent with the guidelines for names of **falls** and **rivers.** Lowercase *upper* or *lower* if the term merely describes that part of one lake: "Fish the *upper lake* in August."

lakebed

lakefront (n., adj.)

lakeshore

lakeside

lama/llama A *lama* is a Buddhist monk; a *llama* is a South American pack animal.

L'Amour, Louis (1908–1988) author of Western novels.

land- Compounds that begin with *land* are generally written as one word: *landfill, landform, landholding, landlocked, landmark, land-*

mass, landowner, landscape, landslide. Exceptions: *land bridge, land grant, land rush.*

-land(s) Compounds that end in *land(s)* are generally written as one word: *badlands, bottomland, flatland, woodland.* Do not overuse to create new words.

landslide (n.)

Land Rover There is no longer a hyphen in this make of vehicle, although the form *Land-Rover* may be appropriate in historical references.

laptop one word

largemouth one word when referring to the fish: *largemouth bass.*

lariat

LaSal Mountains (Utah) not *La Sal Mountains;* but the town is *La Sal.*

Lassen Peak not *Mount Lassen.*

lasso, lassos

last-ditch (adj.)

Latino/Latina See **Hispanic** and **ethnicity.**

latitude lowercase; **parallel** is also lowercase: *the 38th parallel.* Also see **longitude.**

Latter-day Saints The full name of the Mormon Church is *Church of Jesus Christ of Latter-day Saints.*

lava tube

lay, lie The verb *lay* takes an object: chickens *lay* eggs. Past tense: *laid.* The verb *lie* does not take an object. After that 15-mile hike, I wanted to *lie* down. Past tense: *lay.* After my hike, I *lay* down and took a nap.

layback *lieback* preferred for the climbing technique.

lead climbing, lead (v.) "She *leads* 5.10."

-leaf Compounds written as one word: *longleaf, shortleaf.*

lean-to, lean-tos

Leave No Trace Capitalize when referring to the program and principles of Leave No Trace, Inc., a nonprofit educational organization: *a booklet on Leave No Trace practices.* We prefer zero-impact as the generic equivalent.

Leeper Z a brand of piton.

leeward

left-hand, right-hand (adj.)

leftmost, rightmost (adj.) one word, like *hindmost* and *innermost*.

-legged a *four-legged* creature.

Leica camera.

lek(s) (n.) territory of a male animal during breeding season, such as the ground on which a bird displays.

lemon yellow

Leopold, Aldo (1886–1948) ecologist, author of *A Sand County Almanac.*

less Hyphenate a compound before the noun: a *less-traveled* road. No hyphen after the noun: this road is *less traveled.* No hyphen when *less* is a suffix, unless the preceding word ends in the letter "l": *roadless, trackless.*

levee/levy A *levee* is an embankment; a *levy* is a tax.

Levi's jeans.

Lewis, Captain Meriwether (1774–1809) leader, with **William Clark,** of the Lewis and Clark Expedition.

Lewis and Clark Expedition Capitalize, as the name of a historically significant expedition.

lieback preferred over *layback.*

life as the second element in a compound: *bird life, plant life,* but *wildlife.*

life cycle

life jacket, life preserver, life vest

life span

lifestyle preferred over *life-style* or *life style.*

life zone Capitalize terms in the Merriam system, which describes ecological zones in terms of elevation: *Lower Sonoran*

Life Zone, Upper Sonoran Life Zone, Transition Life Zone, Canadian Life Zone, Hudsonian Life Zone, Arctic–Alpine Tundra Life Zone. On second reference, *the life zone, the zone*.

lift ticket

lighthouse, light station capitalize when part of a proper name. The same rule applies to *lightship*, a light station on a ship.

lightning the flash that accompanies thunder; not *lightening*.

lightweight (adj.)

light-year (n.) preferred over *light year*.

-like Compounds that end in *like* are usually written as one word: insectlike. Use a hyphen if the word ends in one or two l's: *funnel-like, bell-like*. Also hyphenate if the word is a proper noun or has three or more syllables: *Jeep-like, cathedral-like*.

like, as, such as *Like* is a preposition, which takes an object: He runs *like* a gazelle. *As* is a conjunction: He runs *as* a gazelle does. *Like* and *such as* are interchangeable when giving an example: *wildflowers such as arnica* or *wildflowers like arnica*.

lilypad

limb, limn A *limb* is a branch, or an arm or a leg; to *limn* is to describe or paint a picture.

limited-access highway

Linderman, Frank Bird (1869–1938) Montana writer.

Lisa, Manuel (1772?–1820) important figure in the fur trade; formed the Missouri Fur Company.

little In compounds before a noun, hyphenate: a *little-known* destination. After a noun, do not hyphenate: This destination is *little known*.

Little Bighorn the river and the battle.

Little Bighorn Battlefield National Monument not *Custer Battlefield*.

littoral (adj.) of the seashore; intertidal.

live oak a species (not the condition of the oak).

llama See usage note at **lama/llama**.

Llano Estacado an area of southeastern New Mexico, west Texas, and northwestern Oklahoma. Do not italicize. Also known as the **Staked Plains**.

loblolly, loblolly pine

loch/lock A *loch* is a Scottish lake; canals have *locks*.

Loctite a brand of adhesives.

lode a vein of ore, as in *Comstock Lode, mother lode;* not *load,* a weight or burden.

lodge Capitalize when part of a proper name: *Bryce Canyon Lodge, the lodge.*

lodgepole pine

loggerhead turtle not *loggerhead sea turtle.*

logjam

long- Compound adjectives are usually hyphenated: *long-sought, long-term, long-winded.* Compound nouns are usually written as two words: *long run, long shot, long term.* No hyphen in the phrase *in the long term.*

long distance (n.), **long-distance** (adj., adv.)

longhorn referring to cattle.

longhouse one word for the style of American Indian architecture.

longitude In stating longitude, the word *meridian* is lowercase: *the 180th meridian.*

long johns

longleaf (adj.) as in *longleaf pine.*

long-sleeve or **long-sleeved** Either is acceptable, depending on author preference; but should be consistent with other similar terms in the text: *a long-sleeved shirt and a wide-brimmed hat.*

Longs Peak (Colorado) no apostrophe.

long-time (adj.) preferred over *longtime.*

look-see (n.)

lost arrow a kind of thin piton.

Lost Coast (California)

Louisiana Purchase

lower Capitalize when considered part of a proper name: the *Lower Peninsula* (Michigan) but the *lower forty-eight states.*

lowland(s)

low-lying (adj.)

lugsail(s) (n.)

Luhan, Mabel Dodge (1879–1962) writer, friend of artists, and famous resident of Taos, New Mexico. Not *Lujan.*

Luhr Jensen & Sons, Inc. manufacturer of lures: *a Luhr Jensen Kwikfish.*

lumbar/lumber *Lumbar* relates to the lower back (as in a *lumbar pack*), *lumber* is wood.

lures See **flies and lures.**

luxuriant means "lush," as in *luxuriant vegetation;* not *luxurious,* "sumptuous."

-ly When an adverb ending in *-ly* modifies an adjective, there is no hyphen between the words: *federally owned land.*

Lycra a brand of **spandex** (**spandex** is not a trademark).

Lyell, Sir Charles (1797–1875) British geologist whose *Principles of Geology* influenced Darwin.

Lyme disease

lynx (sing., pl.), **kitten**

M

machete

Mackenzie Mountains, Mackenzie River, Mackenzie District (Northwest Territories, Canada)

Mackinac Island (Michigan), **Straits of Mackinac** Use the spelling *mackinaw* to refer to the coat or blanket; also *Mackinaw River* (Illinois).

Maclean, Norman (1902–1990) author of *Young Men and Fire* and *A River Runs Through It, and Other Stories.*

madrone or **madroño** Follow regional usage.

maelstrom

magazine Lowercase the word *magazine* unless it is actually part of the title: an article in *Backpacker* magazine. Better: an article in *Backpacker.*

Magnum Capitalize: *a .44-caliber Magnum.* Also see **caliber.**

mainmast, mainsail, mainsheet

main stem of a river.

mal de mer seasickness. No need to italicize.

mallard, mallards, drake, hen, duckling

malpais lava badlands, as at El Malpais National Monument, New Mexico. Not italicized.

Manifest Destiny

manmade (adj.) not *man-made;* artificial or manufactured preferred

mano a grinding stone; the grinding surface is a **metate.** Neither term is italicized.

mantel/mantle A *mantel* is found over a fireplace. In rock climbing, to *mantel* is to lift oneself up onto a mantel-like ledge. A *mantle* is a cloak, as in "a *mantle* of snow covered the ground." Coleman-type lanterns use *mantles,* so called because of their shape. Also: *kernmantle* rope, made of a core and a sheath.

Mantle is also the geological term for the part of the earth between the crust and the core.

manzanita

maps Capitalize (and italicize) the name of a map if there is a clear formal title: the Automobile Club of Southern California's *Guide to Indian Country.* If the exact title is composed of many parts, an acceptable form (all in roman type) is *the Trails Illustrated map of the Grand Gulch area.* Refer to U.S. Geological Survey quads by the names shown on the maps, in roman type: *Bluff NW quad.*

Note: A book page that contains only a map should not show a running head.

mare's-tail an aquatic plant.

Maritime Provinces (Canada) the provinces of New Brunswick, Nova Scotia, and Prince Edward Island.

marlin/marline a *marlin* is a fish; a *marline* is a kind of rope used in boating.

marlinespike used in splicing rope.

marmot(s) short-legged, burrowing rodents. **Woodchucks,** sometimes called **groundhogs,** are *marmots.*

marshland(s)

marsh mallow/marshmallow A *marsh mallow* is a plant; a *marshmallow* is a sugary confection.

marten, martens a small mammal resembling a weasel; not *martin,* a kind of bird.

martin a kind of swallow (the bird); not *marten,* a small mammal.

Mason-Dixon Line the southern border of Pennsylvania, considered the boundary between North and South.

MasterCard

masterful/masterly *Masterful* means "behaving like a master," i.e., in a commanding way. *Masterly* means "skillful": a *masterly* climber.

Mauna Kea, Mauna Loa *Mauna* means "mountain," so avoid redundancy.

May, Karl (1842–1912) popular German author of Western novels.

mayday a call for help. *May Day* is the first of May.

mayfly

McDonald's the fast food chain.

meadowland(s)

meadowlark

medals Olympic medals are lowercase, as are Olympic events. *She won two gold medals; she is an Olympic gold medalist; the silver medal in the giant slalom.*

medevac not *medivac.*

meltwater (n.)

Mepps manufacturer of *Mepps Black Fury* and other lures.

Mercator projection

Mercurochrome a trademark for a kind of antiseptic.

meridian lowercase; used to name longitudes: *the 180th meridian.*

merit badge Lowercase this term and the subject for which it is awarded by the Boy Scouts or Girl Scouts: *a merit badge in archery.*

mesa or **tableland** Follow local practice to determine which word to use (*mesa* is used more commonly). Capitalize when part of a proper name: *White Mesa,* but *the mesa* on second reference. Also see **butte.**
On the Hopi Reservation: *First Mesa, Second Mesa, Third Mesa.*

mesatop

mesquite

metate a grinding surface; see **mano.** Not italicized.

Meteor Crater Capitalize, and do not precede with "the," when referring to the site in Coconino County, Arizona. Also known as *Barringer Crater,* but *Meteor Crater* is the official name.

Métis of mixed French-Canadian and American Indian ancestry.

Metolius manufacturer of climbing gear.

metroplex Lowercase: *the Dallas metroplex.*

Mexican American (n.), **Mexican-American** (adj.)

Mexico The states of Mexico: Aguascalientes, Baja California, Baja California Sur, Campeche, Chiapas, Chihuahua, Coahuila, Colima, Durango, Guanajuato, Guerrero, Hidalgo, Jalisco, México, Michoacán, Morelos, Nayarit, Nuevo León, Oaxaca, Puebla, Querétaro, Quintana Roo, San Luis Potosí, Sinaloa, Sonora, Tabasco, Tamaulipas, Tlaxcala, Veracruz, Yucatán, and Zacatecas.

micro- Compounds beginning with this prefix are written as one word: *microchip, microenvironment, microfiber, microfleece, microorganism.*

mid- Compounds beginning with *mid* have no hyphen unless a capitalized word follows: *midair, midday, midrib, midsummer, midwinter, mid-July.*

midden a trash pile, especially one at an archaeological site. Also called a **kitchen midden.**

Middle Atlantic or **Mid-Atlantic states** are New York, New Jersey, and Pennsylvania.

midnight sun

Midwest Capitalize the region, *the Midwest,* and its people, *Midwesterners.* Also capitalize the adjective describing the region, *Midwestern,* as in *a Midwestern city.*
For the Midwestern states, see regions of the **United States.**

Migratory Bird Hunting and Conservation Stamp informally known as the *Duck Stamp.*

mile Use decimals to indicate fractions of a mile: *1.5 miles, 10.7 miles.* For whole numbers, do not use a decimal unless emphasizing the accuracy of the mileage point: *"At 2.0 mile, turn left onto Forest Road 2023"*; but *"After 2* *miles,* the trail begins to climb."

For distances of less than 1 mile, use the singular: *0.5 mile,* not *0.5 miles.* Always use a zero before the decimal. When writing directions, *"at* x miles" should be reserved for mileage counts made from the starting point, and *"in* x miles" for incremental mileages between points mentioned in the directions. Thus, "From the Clark Fork Bridge in Missoula, head east. *At 5.5 miles,* turn left onto Holofernes Road. *In another 2 miles,* turn right onto Reserve Boulevard."

When approximating distances of less than a mile, write out *a quarter of a mile, a third of a mile, half a mile,* preceded by the word *about,* instead of *about 0.5 mile* or *about 0.33 mile.* The same principle applies to approximations of **time.**

mile marker, milepost Lowercase and use numerals, without the # symbol or abbreviation *No.:* Turn right on the dirt road just past *mile marker 17.*

milfoil a plant.

military titles In text and captions, spell out military titles: *Lieutenant Colonel George Armstrong Custer,* not *Lt. Col.*

Milky Way

Miller, Alfred Jacob (1810–1874) artist known for his paintings of mountain men.

millimeters Abbreviate *mm,* with no period and no hyphen between the numeral and the abbreviation: *a 10 mm rope, 6 mm cord, 35 mm film, 9 mm pistol.* For clarity, spell out a number that precedes a measurement: *Take two 10 mm ropes.* Note: To avoid ambiguity, measurements in inches or feet take a hyphen before the noun: *a 150-foot rope.*

Mimbres a stage of the Mogollon Indian culture, known for beautiful pottery. Adjective form: *Mimbreño.*

minable (adj.) preferred over *mineable;* means "capable of being mined."

mine Capitalize the word *mine* when part of a proper name: *Bingham Canyon Copper Mine.* Lowercase when used descriptively, as with mines that are known by one name: *the*

Speculator, or *the Speculator mine.*

mineral A *mineral* occurs naturally and has a definite chemical composition; *rock* is an aggregate of minerals; *stone* is earth and/or mineral(s) that are formed into a mass, producing a substance like *sandstone* or *mudstone.* Also see **rock, stone.**

Mining Law of 1872

minivan

mink (sing., pl.), kit

minute With U.S. Geological Survey topo maps: *7.5-minute series, 15-minute series.*

Mirrolure a brand of lures. Not *Mirrorlure.*

mission Capitalize in a name: *Mission San Juan Bautista;* but *the mission, the California missions.*

mistletoe

mistral the French wind.

mixed-grass prairie

mm no period after the abbreviation for **millimeters.** Also see **film** and **guns.**

mobile home

moccasin

mochila Spanish, but no need to italicize when referring to the mailbag carried by pony express riders. Not *mochilla.*

Mogollon Rim

mogul lowercase for the bump on a ski slope; capitalized, *Mogul* refers to a dynasty in the country of India.

Mohave, Mojave *Mojave* is the typical spelling in California: *Mojave Desert; Mojave,* the town in Kern County; *Mojave River. Mohave* is the typical spelling in Arizona: *Mohave County, Mohave Point* (at the Grand Canyon), but *Mojave City,* Arizona. Indian tribes: Fort McDowell *Mohave-Apache* Community of the Fort McDowell Indian Reservation, Arizona; *Fort Mojave* Indian Tribe of Arizona, California, and Nevada.

moki, moqui, mokee a former term for the **Anasazi** or

Ancestral Puebloan people; sometimes appears in historical references. Still appears in some place names, as in the *Moki Dugway* (Utah), and in the informal term *moki steps*, Anasazi handholds and footholds cut into cliffs. Spellings vary in place names.

moleskin lowercase.

Möllhausen, Heinrich B. (1825–1905) German traveler, artist on various surveys of the West; known for drawings of the Grand Canyon.

money If you can write the amount and the word *dollars* in two words, write it out: *five dollars, fifty dollars.* Exception: in guidebooks, use only numerals: *$5, $50.*
If the amount plus the word *dollars* is three or more words, use numerals and the dollar sign: *$55, $100* (not *$100.00*), *$5.75.*
The same rules apply to amounts in cents (use the dollar sign, not the cents sign): *fifty cents,* but *$.98,* not *98¢* or *ninety-eight cents.*
The same rules apply to forms of currency of other countries.

monofilament used for fishing line.

monopod a one-legged support for a camera; a *monopode* is a living thing that has only one foot.

monopoint crampon feature.

Monterey, the Monterey Peninsula (California)

Monterrey (Mexico)

Montreal no accent.

monument capitalize when part of a proper name: *the Four Corners Monument,* but *the monument* on second reference.

moon lowercase: "The *moon* rose at 7:00."

moonlight (n.)

moonlit (adj.)

moonrise (n.), **moonset** (n.)

moose (sing., pl.), bull, cow, calf

moraine earth and rock deposited by a melting glacier. A *terminal moraine* marks the farthest edge of a glacier's advance.

Moran, Thomas (1837–1926) American artist (born in England) known for his paintings of Yellowstone.

more than Use *more than* instead of *over* to indicate a greater number: "There are *more than* 200 million people in the United States." Similarly, use *fewer* instead of *under*. Always use *fewer*, not *less*, when referring to specific numbers rather than a general amount: *fewer dollars*, but *less money*. Exception: When copy editing, do not change a casual expression such as "It's just *over* a mile to the camp" to "It's just *more than* a mile to the camp."

morel a kind of mushroom; *morellos* are sour cherries.

Mormon tea

Mormon Trail

morph a form of appearance of a species: *light morph ferruginous hawk.*

mosquito, mosquitoes

-most One word, no hyphen: *hindmost, innermost, leftmost, rightmost.*

Motel 6

mother lode not *load.*

Mother Nature Capitalize (although use of such personification is discouraged).

motion sickness

motor home

motor inn, motor lodge

motor scooter

motor vehicle

motte small cluster of trees on a prairie (regional Western usage): *an oak motte.*

Mound Builders the prehistoric Indians who built mounds throughout the Midwest and South. Capitalize names of individual mounds and groups of mounds: *the Cahokia Mounds, Monks Mound.*

mount, mountains Capitalize and spell out when part of a
proper name: *Rocky Mountains, Mount of the Holy Cross, Mount
Rainier,* but *the mountain(s)* on second reference.
Use the complete name on first reference: *the Crazy Mountains.*
Short forms are okay on second reference: *the Crazies.*
Nicknames, such as *Baldy,* are okay on second reference
(but use the full name for the first reference in a caption).
Do not put quotation marks around such nicknames.
Okay to abbreviate *Mt., Mts.* on maps and in captions.

mountain bike, mountain biker, mountain biking a mountain
bike is nonmotorized. See **trail bike.**

The Mountaineers with a capital *The.* Their monthly publication
is called *The Mountaineer.*

mountain goat, mountain goats, billy, nanny, kid

mountain lion (or **cougar** or **puma**), **mountain lions, cub** or
kitten Don't write *mountain lion* on one page and *puma* on the
next; use only one term in a text to avoid confusion. Use the
term most common in the region.

mountain man Lowercase references to the annual nineteenth-
century *mountain man rendezvous.*

mountain range

mountain sheep

mountain sickness also **altitude sickness.**

**mountain standard time (MST), mountain daylight time
(MDT)**

mountaintop

Mountie preferred over *Mounty.* Nickname for a member of the
Royal Canadian Mounted Police.

mourning dove Not *morning dove.*

mouse, mice Also *field mouse, field mice.*

mud Most animal names that begin with *mud* are two words:
mud hen, mud minnow, mud puppy, mud snake, mud turtle, mud wasp.

mud flat

mudflow (n.)

mud pot

mudslide

mudstone

Muir, John (1838–1914) naturalist and conservationist.

mukluk

mule *20-mule team.*

mule deer

muleskinner a *muleteer;* but *muleskinner* is more common in a Western context.

Mullan, Captain John (1830–1909), builder of the Mullan Road, finished in 1863.

mullein not *mullen.*

multi- Compounds beginning with this prefix are generally written as one word: *multicultural, multidirectional, multimedia, multipitch.* When the second word begins with a vowel, hyphenated is preferred for ease of reading: *multi-agency, multi-use.*

mummy bag

Münter hitch a friction knot. Not *Munter.*

museum Capitalize when part of a proper name: *the American Museum of Fly Fishing, the Museum of the Rockies,* but *the fly fishing museum, the museum.*
Titles of museum exhibits are capitalized and italicized: *Crossing the Frontier: Photographs of the Developing West, 1849 to the Present* at the San Francisco Museum of Modern Art. *Art of the Southern Cheyenne* at the Plains Indian Museum. But roman type for *an exhibit on art of the Southern Cheyenne.*

muskeg a bog, especially in northern regions.

muskellunge a species of fish; *muskie* acceptable on second reference.

musk ox, musk oxen not *muskox.* In the Bovidae family, the same family as domestic cattle, sheep, and goats. They live in the tundra of the far north.

muskrat, muskrats

Mustad manufacturer of fishing tackle.

mustang a wild horse, in the American West.

Muybridge, Eadweard (1830–1904) photographer known for motion studies and photographs of Yosemite.

mycology the study of fungi.

Mylar a trademark.

myotis a genus of bats. Capitalize and italicize when part of the scientific name: *Myotis auriculus.* Lowercase, roman type when used as part of a common name, such as *southwestern myotis.*

myriad can be a noun or an adjective: *a myriad of stars filled the night sky,* or *myriad stars.*

N

Nalgene

names of animals, plants, etc. See entries at **animal names, plant names,** and **rock and land.** Also see **taxonomy** and **Names and Capitalization, p. 16.**

Nansen, Fridtjof (1861–1930) Norwegian Arctic explorer.

narrow gauge (n.), **narrow-gauge** (adj.) *a narrow-gauge railway.*

narrows Capitalize when considered part of a proper name: *the Narrows of Zion Canyon, the Narrows.* Note: This guideline is consistent with the guidelines for **falls** and **rivers.** Lowercase when used descriptively: "There is a take-out a mile before *the narrows* of this river."

nation Capitalize when used with the name of an Indian tribe: *the Navajo Nation,* but *the nation.*

National Champion Tree a designation of the group American Forests, meaning that the tree has been listed on the National Register of Big Trees. Handle as an award, and capitalize: This gigantic pecan is a *National Champion Tree.*

National Climbing Classification System

national conservation area a BLM designation. Capitalize when part of a full name: *Red Rock Canyon National Conservation Area.* Lowercase when used alone.

National Environmental Policy Act of 1970 (NEPA)

National Estuarine Research Reserve System administered by the National Oceanic and Atmospheric Administration (NOAA), part of the U.S. Department of Commerce. *Apalachicola National Estuarine Research Reserve, the Apalachicola reserve.*

national forest Capitalize only when used as part of a proper name: *Helena National Forest*. No hyphen when used as a compound adjective: *national forest land*. Use both words, not just *forest*, when referring to something on, in, or belonging to a national forest: *a national forest boundary*.

National Fresh Water Fishing Hall of Fame *Fresh Water* is two words. Not *Hall of Fame and Museum*.

National Geographic Society publishes *National Geographic,* the magazine.

national grasslands are administered by the USDA Forest Service and are part of the National Forest System. Capitalize when part of the name: *Buffalo Gap National Grasslands* in South Dakota, but *a national grasslands, the grasslands*.

national historic landmark Landmarks are listed on the National Register of Historic Places, which is administered by the National Park Service (not the **National Trust for Historic Preservation**). Lowercase except when capitalization is desirable to avoid ambiguity or highlight the term as an official designation.

national marine sanctuary Sanctuaries are administered by the National Oceanic and Atmospheric Administration (NOAA), part of the U.S. Department of Commerce. Capitalize in a name: *Monterey Bay National Marine Sanctuary*. Lowercase when the term stands alone: Monterey Bay is a *national marine sanctuary*.

national natural landmark Landmarks are designated by the secretary of the interior upon the recommendation of the National Park System. Landmarks are listed on the **National Registry of Natural Landmarks** (not "Register"). Lowercase, except when capitalization is desirable to avoid ambiguity or highlight the term as an official designation: The Gingko Petrified Forest is a *national natural landmark*.

National Outdoor Leadership School *NOLS* acceptable on second reference.

national park Capitalize only when part of a proper name: *Yellowstone National Park,* but *the national park*. On second reference: *Yellowstone,* not *Yellowstone Park*.

Note: The National Park Service sometimes capitalizes *Park* in its publications: "Firearms are not permitted in the *Park*." If necessary, consult with a National Park Service representative for a particular park's preferred usage.

Capitalize *System* when referring to the *National Park System* or the *Wild and Scenic Rivers System.*

Capitalize units of national parks: the *Needles District* of Canyonlands National Park. Also capitalize such terms as the *South Entrance* to Yellowstone National Park, in keeping with National Park Service style.

National Park Service Abbreviate *NPS*, not *Park Service.*

national recreation area Capitalize when part of a name: *Glen Canyon National Recreation Area,* but *a national recreation area.* The abbreviation *NRA* is acceptable on second reference.

National Register of Historic Places the list of **national historic landmarks,** historic areas of national parks, and other historic properties; list maintained by the National Park Service.

National Scenic Byway a designation of the Federal Highway Administration (different program from the BLM's National Back Country Byway Program and the USDA Forest Service's scenic byways). Roads can be designated *All-American Roads, National Scenic Byways,* or *State Scenic Byways.* Capitalize these terms when referring to them as designations, and when they appear as part of names: *Native American Scenic Byway.* Lowercase when used descriptively: *Utah 12 is a state scenic byway.*

National Ski Patrol a national organization whose members belong to local **ski patrols.**

National Trust for Historic Preservation a nonprofit organization, not a government agency.

National Watchable Wildlife Program a multi-agency program, led by Defenders of Wildlife.

National Weather Service or *the weather service* (lowercase); not *U.S. Weather Bureau,* the former name.

National Wetlands Inventory a program of the U.S. Fish and

Wildlife Service; maps wetlands.

National Wilderness Preservation System

national wildlife refuge Capitalize when part of a proper name: *Cibola National Wildlife Refuge,* but *a national wildlife refuge.*

Native American The terms *American Indian* or *Indian* are preferred. *Alaska Native* is the preferred term for native peoples of Alaska. Also see **Indian.**

Native American Church Capitalize when referring to the organized religion.

Native American Graves Protection and Repatriation Act of 1990 (NAGPRA)

natural anchor, natural gear

natural history

Navajo, Navajos not *Navaho, Navahos,* although that spelling may appear in titles or historical references: Laura Gilpin's *The Enduring Navaho.*

Navajo flu Do not use; the correct name is **hantavirus.**

navy See **armed forces.**

neap tide

nearshore (adj.)

necropsy an autopsy performed on an animal: "Biologists *necropsied* the grizzly bear."

neo- Compounds beginning with *neo,* which means "new," are generally written as one word: *Neolithic, neophyte, neoprene, neotropical.* Exception: use a hyphen when the word that follows *neo* begins with a capital letter: *neo-Darwinian.*

neoprene lowercase.

névé (n.) a field of snow at the upper end of a glacier; or, more generally, a field of old snow.

never-ending (adj.)

New England comprises Connecticut, Maine, Massachusetts, New Hampshire, Rhode Island, and Vermont.

newspaper names Italicize, but do not italicize or capitalize a preliminary "The" in running text: *a country inn featured in the Salt Lake Tribune.*

New World

Nez Perce (sing., pl.) not *Nez Percé.*

night Compound nouns with *night* are often written as one word: *nightfall, nighthawk, nightjar, nighttime.* Exceptions: *night crawler, night heron.*

Nikon

Ninemile one word in Montana place names.

nisei, nisei second-generation Japanese Americans, the children of **issei.** Lowercase, roman type.

no man's land (n.) no hyphens.

non- Unless the word that follows begins with a capital letter, compounds with *non* are written as one word, whether noun or adjective: *nonfiction, nonnative, nonprofit.* But note: *persona non grata.*

nongame (adj.)

Nordic skiing Refers to any kind of skiing in which the binding leaves the heel loose, as in ski jumping or **cross-country skiing.**

nor'easter (n.) a storm coming from the northeast.

north, northern Directional terms are lowercase: *northernmost, north-northwest, northern Montana.* Capitalize when part of a term commonly used to refer to a region: *Northern California, the Northern Rockies, the Pacific Northwest.*
Capitalize *northern* when part of the name of an Indian tribe, whether the tribe's current formal name or in historical references: *the Northern Cheyenne.*

northbound

north-central (adj.) with a hyphen; but *northeast, northwest.*

norther (n.) a storm from the north.

northern lights or **aurora borealis**

Northern Pacific Railway

Northern Rockies the part of the Rocky Mountains in Idaho, Montana, and Wyoming; can also include the **Canadian Rockies.**

North Pole

North Shore on Hawaii; also on Long Island.

North Slope (Alaska)

North Star or **Polaris**

Northwest Northern California, Oregon, Washington (the **Pacific Northwest**) plus Idaho and western Montana.

Northwest Passage

Northwest Territories (Canada)

North Woods Capitalize when referring to the region of mixed conifer and hardwood forest in the Northeast and Upper Midwest.

Norway spruce

no-see-um a small biting fly.

noseplug

numbers and numerals See **Numbers,** p. 27.

number one (n., adj.)

Nunavut Territory a new Canadian territory, beginning in 1999. Formed by the splitting of the Northwest Territories into two. The eastern part is Nunavut. The postal abbreviation for both territories is *NT.*

nut(s) also chocks or wedges. Capitalize *Stoppers,* a trademark.

nuthatch

nutria an aquatic rodent, resembling a **muskrat.** Also known as **coypu.**

nymph the larval form of some insects.

O

oarlock

oasis, oases

observatory Follow the rules for **buildings,** and capitalize when part of a proper noun: *Lowell Observatory, the observatory.*

ocean Capitalize when part of a name, lowercase when standing alone: *the Atlantic Ocean, the Atlantic,* but *the ocean.*

oceanfront

oceangoing (adj.)

ocher preferred over *ochre.*

ocotillo, ocotillos

octopus, octopuses preferred over *octopi* for plural.

off Adjectives with *off* are often hyphenated: *off-peak, off-road.* Exception: *offbeat.*

off-hand in rock climbing, a crack wider than a climber's fingers but not wide enough for a hand jam; not *offhand,* "casual."

off-limits (adj.)

off-piste

off-ramp

off-road vehicle

off-season (n., adj., adv.)

offshore (adj., adv.)

off-site (adj., adv.)

off-the-seat (adj., adv.)

off-trail (adj.) as in *off-trail hiking.*

off-width crack, or **off-width** (n.) in climbing, a crack wider than a **hand jam** but smaller than a **chimney** (usually about 3.5 to 8 inches wide).

OHV off-highway vehicle. Do not use unless preferred by the agency administering the area described. In that case, use the abbreviation only on second reference.

oil field

Okanagan, Okanogan The *Okanagan River* in British Columbia becomes the *Okanogan River* on the United States side of the border. *Okanagan Lake,* British Columbia; but *Okanogan,* the county and town in Washington State.

okay not *OK.*

O'Keeffe, Georgia (1887–1986) American artist known for paintings of flowers and Western landscapes.

Okefenokee Swamp

Oklahoma land rush

old *a three-year-old tent. The tent is three years old. A camping trip for ten-year-olds.*

Old Faithful

old growth (n.), **old-growth** (adj.) *old-growth forest*

old-time (adj.), **old-timer** (n.)

Old West

oleoresin capsicum lowercase. The active ingredient in **bear spray/pepper spray.**

Oljato, Oljeto In San Juan County, Utah: *Oljato Trading Post, Oljato Wash,* not *Oljeto* (but the name of the USGS quad is, confusingly, *Oljeto,* and that spelling may appear in historical references).

olla a pottery water jug.

Olympics Capitalize: *the Olympic Games, the Olympics, the Winter (or Summer) Olympics. An Olympic-sized* pool. Lowercase Olympic events and medals: *an Olympic gold medal, a silver medalist, the bronze medal in giant slalom.*

omnivorous

on to, onto One word in sentences like "walk out *onto* the pier." Two words when *on* is part of a phrasal verb: "They *drove on* to the next town."

on My Mind as in the *America on My Mind* series. A registered trademark of Falcon.

onboard (adj.) preferred over *on-board*.

one-of-a-kind (adj.)

one-way (adj.) *a one-way street.* Two words, no hyphen, for the noun: "There is more than *one way* to the top of the mountain."

on-line as in *on-line resources.*

onshore (adj.)

on-sight (adj., adv.) in rock climbing, describes climbing a route with no prior knowledge or practice.

on-site (adj., adv.)

open-air (adj.), **open air** (n.)

open range (n.)

opossum The short form *possum* (not *'possum*) acceptable in quoted speech.

Oregon Trail

Oriental Now usually considered an offensive term for Asian peoples, cultures, and art. Use a specific nationality. See **ethnicity.**

orienteering

O-ring(s)

ORV off-road vehicle. Do not use unless preferred by the agency administering the area described. In that case, use the abbreviation only on second reference.

osier Hyphenate in *red-osier dogwood.*

O'Sullivan, Timothy (1840?–1882) photographer on many surveys of the West.

otter, otters

out- Compounds that begin with *out* are usually written as
one word: *outboard, outbuilding, outcrop, outfall, outflow, outhouse,
outland, outlaw, outlet, outlier, outmaneuver, outnumber, outrigger,
outtalk, outwash.*

outback lowercase when referring to rural areas of Australia and
New Zealand. The term is comparable to a descriptive term
like *backcountry*, not the name of a region like the *Far West*.

outdoor (adj.), **outdoors** (adv.) or **out-of-doors** (adv.)

outdoorsman, outdoorswoman But note the hyphen in the
name of the program, *Becoming an Outdoors-Woman*.

Outer Banks islands off coast of North Carolina.

outer continental shelf

outerwear

out-of-doors (adv.)

out-of-the-way (adj.)

Outward Bound the organization; but *outward-bound* (adj.).

over- Compounds beginning with *over* are usually written as
one word: *overboard, overcast, overexert, overfish, overgraze, overhang,
overnight, overreact, overseas, overstory, overwinter* (v.).

-over Compounds ending in *over* are usually written as one
word: *flyover, stopover.*

Overland Capitalize the names *Overland Mail Company* and
Overland Stage Line.

Overland Trail

overlook Capitalize when considered part of a proper name,
as in many locations within parks: *Spider Rock Overlook* at
Canyon de Chelly. Follow the usage of the agency that
manages the site.
Lowercase *overlook* when it is used as a descriptive term,
following the complete name of a place: *Inspiration Point, the
Inspiration Point overlook, the overlook at Inspiration Point.*

oviparous (adj.)

owl, owls, owlet

Owyhee the river and mountains in Idaho.

ox, oxen An ox is an adult castrated bull; a steer is castrated before maturity. Also see **cow.**

oxbow (n., adj.) as in *an oxbow lake.* Not *ox-bow.*

oystercatcher the bird.

Ozark Mountains, the Ozarks

Ozark states Arkansas, Missouri, and western Kentucky.

ozone layer lowercase.

P

pac boots have an inner liner.

Pacific coast lowercase when referring to a geographical area: *marine life along the Pacific coast; beaches of the Pacific coast.* Capitalize when referring to a region: *Pacific Coast states,* or, more commonly, *the West Coast.*

Pacific Crest National Scenic Trail, Pacific Crest Trail On second reference, *PCT* is acceptable.

Pacific Flyway

Pacific Northwest Northern California, Oregon, and Washington. The **Northwest** also includes Idaho and Montana west of the Continental Divide.

Pacific standard time (PST), Pacific daylight time (PDT)

pack *horsepacking, mulepacking.*

packhorse

pack ice (n.)

pack rat

pack string general reference to a group of pack animals: Those horses in the pasture are Bob's *pack string.*

pack train a group of pack animals strung together as generally seen on a trail.

paddleboat/pedal boat A *paddleboat* has **paddle wheels;** a *pedal boat* has foot pedals.

paddleboard

paddlesports

paddle wheel, paddle wheeler

Painted Desert

pair, pairs *Pair* can be singular or plural. It is singular when considered as one thing: *a pair of shoes.* (*Two pair of shoes* is not incorrect, but *pairs* is preferred for plural in such cases.) *Pair* is plural when it is considered as two individuals: *a pair of geese fly; a pair of guides work together.*

pair bond (n.)

Palace of the Governors in Santa Fe.

paleo- Words that begin with this prefix, which means "ancient" or "old," are written as one word, with no hyphen: *paleobotany, Paleolithic, paleontology, paleosite.* Exception: *Paleo-Indian* (n., adj.).

palmetto, palmettos also known as **sabal palm.**

Panama hat

Pan-American (adj.) as in *Pan-American Highway.*

pan fish (n.)

Pangaea

panhandle Capitalize in names such as the *Texas Panhandle,* but *the panhandle.*

pannier(s)

panther in southern United States, a **mountain lion.**

papaw or **pawpaw** Use the spelling most common in the region.

Parabolic skis a trademark; the generic term is **shaped skis.**

parallel lowercase when stating latitude: *40th parallel.*

parfleche no accent on the "e."

parish in Louisiana, equivalent to a county: *Caddo Parish, the parish.*

park Capitalize when part of a proper name: *Wildcat Canyon Regional Park, the regional park.* Also see **national park.**

Park Police the *U.S. Park Police, a Park Police officer.*

parkland(s)

Parks Canada

parkway Capitalize when part of the name of a road, but lowercase when it stands alone: *Blue Ridge Parkway, the parkway.*

Partners for Wildlife a U.S. Fish and Wildlife Service program that helps private landowners restore habitat.

paseo Capitalize in full and short forms of road names: *Paseo de Peralta, the Paseo.*

pass Capitalize the name of a pass: *Donner Pass, South Pass,* but *the pass.*

passerine (adj., n.) refers to birds of the order Passeriformes.

patent a kind of land grant; appears in certain place names: *the Waldo Patent.*

patrol the U.S. Border Patrol.

PCB a pollutant; acronym okay on first reference.

PCT acceptable second reference for the **Pacific Crest Trail.**

peal/peel A *peal* is the sound a bell makes; fruits and vegetables are *peeled;* one keeps one's eye *peeled.*

Peale last name of family of American artists in the 1700s and 1800s. Charles Willson (not *Wilson*) Peale (1741–1827) founded the Peale Museum in Philadelphia, which included natural history specimens. Titian Ramsay Peale (1799–1885) accompanied Stephen Long on his expedition to the Upper Missouri.

Peary, Robert E. (1856–1920) Led expedition that reached the North Pole in 1909. Not *Perry,* the last name of several prominent naval officers in the nineteenth century.

peccary, peccaries The **collared peccary** is a piglike mammal found in the desert Southwest, also called **javelina.**

pedal boat See note at **paddleboat.**

pelagic (adj.) of the ocean: *pelagic birds.*

pemmican

peninsula Capitalize when part of a proper name: *the Monterey Peninsula,* but *the peninsula* on second reference. Also: the *Upper Peninsula* and *Lower Peninsula* of Michigan.

penknife, penlight

penstemon not *pentstemon.*

people not *persons.* But *peoples* when referring to more than one cultural group.

People for the Ethical Treatment of Animals, PETA

pepper spray or **bear spray**

percent not *per cent* or *%.* Use numerals: *50 percent, 99 percent.*

Perlon a trademark: *Perlon cord.*

permafrost

Perseid meteor shower

personal flotation device or **PFD**

petiole the stalk of a leaf.

Petrified Forest Capitalize *the Petrified Forest* when referring to the area included in Petrified Forest National Park. Capitalize the names of other petrified forests, but second references to them are lowercase: *the Gingko Petrified Forest, the petrified forest.*

petroglyphs/pictographs *Petroglyphs* are images cut or chipped into rock; *pictographs* are painted. The general term is **rock art.** Lowercase after a place name: *Butler Wash petroglyphs, Horseshoe Canyon petroglyphs.* The names of some well-known panels and individual images are capitalized, however, and set in roman type: the *Great Gallery* in Horseshoe Canyon; *All-American Man.* Do not put quotation marks around such names.

Petzl manufacturer of climbing gear and head lamps. Capitalize trade names such as the *Petzl Grigri,* a belay device.

PFD or **personal flotation device** preferred over *life jacket* or *life vest.*

pH

phalarope

pheasant, pheasants, hen, chick

photo captions Captions should take the form of a complete sentence or sentences and be capitalized and punctuated appropriately: "The moon rises like a hood ornament along the Beartooth Highway."
Captions should be italicized, set in smaller type, or otherwise

distinguished from the main text.

Abbreviations that are undesirable in text (such as *St.* for *Saint*) may appear in captions when space requires.

pica/pika A *pica* is a unit of type measurement, equal to 12 points; a **pika** is a small mammal.

pickleweed

pickup truck

picnic, picnicker, picnicking

Pieps a brand of avalanche beacon.

pigeon, pigeons, squab

pika, pikas a small mammal, related to rabbits and hares, that lives above **timberline;** not **pica,** a unit of type measurement.

Pikes Peak no apostrophe in *Pikes* except in historical references.

pile/fleece *Pile* is the way yarns are looped to produce *fleece,* a kind of fabric. *Fleece* can be either wool or synthetic, although it is generally used now to refer to synthetic fabrics such as **Polarfleece.**

pileated means "crested," as in *pileated woodpecker.*

Pinchot, Gifford (1865–1946) conservationist and forester.

Pine Barrens Capitalize when referring to the region in New Jersey. Lowercase when used as a generic term meaning an area of pine forest on poor, sandy soil.

pineland(s)

pine marten a furbearing member of the weasel family, resembling **mink** and **fisher.**

pinewood(s) a general term. Capitalize *Pineywoods,* a region of Texas.

piney (adj.) smelling of pine; preferred over *piny.*

piñon pine or **pinyon pine** Use the preferred local spelling.

piñon-juniper woodland or **pinyon-juniper woodland**

piranha

pirogue a kind of dugout canoe.

piste, off-piste Not italicized.

pistil/pistol A *pistil* is the female part of a flower; a *pistol* is a gun.

pitch the part of a climb between belays, usually one rope-length. In climbing guidebooks, use numerals: an *8-pitch* climb; the climb has *8 pitches.* No hyphen in *multipitch.*

pitch-dark (adj.)

pitcher plant

pithouse

piton

pit zips underarm zippers on a jacket; in the form *PitZips,* a trademark of Marmot.

place name not *place-name.*

the Plains when referring to the **Great Plains.**

planetarium capitalize when part of a name: *the Taylor Planetarium,* but *the planetarium at the Museum of the Rockies.*

planets Capitalize their names: *Mars, Venus, the rings of Saturn.* Capitalize *Earth* in the context of other planets, otherwise lowercase, as when used as a synonym for "world": "Yellowstone has more geysers than anywhere else *on earth.*"

plant names Names that end in *berry, brush, root, weed,* and *wort* are almost always written as one word: *cloudberries, rabbitbrush, jimsonweed.* Names that end in *grass* can be one word or two: *bluegrass, bunch grass.*
Common nouns are lowercase except for words that are proper: *arnica; Indian paintbrush.* For scientific names, see **taxonomy.**

plateau, plateaus Capitalize when considered part of a proper name: *the Colorado Plateau, the plateau.*

plate tectonics

playa in the Southwest, a dry **lakebed,** sometimes holding water seasonally.

playboat, playhole

Plexiglas a trademark; *plexiglass* generally.

plunge-step (n., v.)

plurals See names of animals at individual entries.

pluton igneous rock.

Plymouth, Plymouth Rock

P.M., A.M. Small caps, with no space between the elements: 6 A.M. (not 6:00 A.M.), 5:30 P.M., *open from 1 to 4:30 P.M.* Also see **time.**

pocketknife

pocket-sized not *pocketsize.*

pocosin term for an upland swamp, a certain kind of wetland found in the southeastern United States.

pod a group of whales.

-pod Compounds ending in *pod,* which means "foot," are written as one word: *monopod, tripod.*

point a *six-point* bull elk, *12-point* crampons.

poison ivy, poison oak, poison sumac

pokeberry, pokeweed

polar bear

polar cap

Polarfleece, Polartec trademarks, so must be capitalized. Note that *Polarfleece* is one word.

Polaroid a trademark.

polder(s) reclaimed lowland(s) surrounded by dikes. The term is usually used of the Netherlands, but is also used regionally in the United States.

pole *the North Pole, the South Pole, the pole, polar.*

Pole Star Polaris, or the North Star.

pollen, pollination, pollinate

polyethylene

polypropylene often called *polypro* for short.

poncho, ponchos

ponderosa pine

pontoon

pony express lowercase.

porcupine, porcupines, porcupettes

port, starboard *Port* is the left-hand side of a ship (as you face forward); *starboard* is the right-hand side.

portage (n., v.) to carry a canoe, kayak, or bike around an obstacle or from one waterway to the next.

portaledge lowercase, no hyphen.

porthole

posthole (n., v.) refers to hiking in snow, so that holes are left where one has stepped.

post office lowercase.

post office box In an address, abbreviate *P.O. Box* (no space between the abbreviated letters).

potbelly stove preferred over *potbellied stove*; never *pot-bellied*.

pothole

pothunter, pothunting

potsherd preferred over *potshard*; but *shard* preferred over *sherd*.

pound a *400-pound* bear; the bear weighed *400 pounds.*

pour-off (n.)

Powell, John Wesley (1834–1902) explorer of the Colorado River, later head of the U.S. Geological Survey.

PowerBar

power line

powwow

prairie-chicken with a hyphen.

prairie dog, prairie dog town no hyphen.

pray/prey *praying mantis,* but *birds of prey.*

praying mantis, mantises The family name is **mantids.**

pre- Compounds beginning with *pre* are generally written as one word: *predawn, preempt, prehistoric, prewar.* If the word that

follows *pre* begins with an "e," as in *preempt*, it is acceptable to hyphenate *pre-empt;* but this should be consistent.
Also hyphenate if the second word begins with a capital letter: *pre-Columbian.* But *Precambrian*, not *pre-Cambrian*, for the geological term.

precipitate (adj.)**/precipitous** (adj.) *Precipitate* means "hasty" or "reckless"; an accident might be caused by a *precipitate* climber. *Precipitous* means "steep": a mesa with *precipitous* sides.

predacious preferred over *predaceous.*

preserves and sanctuaries Capitalize such terms when part of a proper name: *Año Nuevo State Reserve, Richardson Bay Audubon Sanctuary, Bolinas Lagoon Preserve.* Lowercase when the terms stand alone: *the Audubon sanctuary.*

Presidents' Day

Primaloft a trademark for a kind of insulation.

primeval/primordial These words are not interchangeable. *Primeval* means "ancient": "This is the forest *primeval.*" *Primordial* means "first in order": "Many *primordial* life forms are now extinct."

Prince Edward Island one of the Maritime Provinces of Canada.

principal/principle *Principal* can be a noun or an adjective. As a noun, it means a most important person: the *principal* of a school. As an adjective, *principal* means "of primary importance": Her *principal* goal was to save the redwoods. *Principle* is always a noun, never an adjective, and means "basic rule": the *principles* of avalanche avoidance.

prizes Capitalize the full, formal names of specific prizes but not general terms like *first prize* or *gold medal.* Capitalize the word *prize* only if it is part of the formal name of an award. Also see **medals.**

pronghorn, pronghorn, buck, doe, fawn

province Lowercase the word *province* when used as part of a geological term (but the name of the province is capitalized in geological style): *Basin and Range province, Ridge and Valley*

province.
Capitalize when part of a proper name: *Maritime Provinces.*
Lowercase preceding the name: *the province of Alberta.*

provincial park in Canada, a park administered by a province.
Capitalize when part of the name: *Clearwater River Provincial Park,* but *a provincial park.*

prusik lowercase. A kind of friction knot.

pseudo- Compounds that begin with this prefix are generally written as one word: *pseudomorph, pseudonym, pseudoscience.*

psi pounds per square inch.

ptarmigan

pueblito(s) small pueblos, specifically those settlements of Pueblo Indians in the 1700s in the *Dinetah,* the Navajo region of northwestern New Mexico.

pueblo Capitalize when referring to a pueblo as a place: *Laguna Pueblo, Taos Pueblo,* but *the pueblo, an Indian pueblo.* Also capitalize when referring to the names of Pueblo tribes as administrative entities or when referring in general to Pueblo Indian tribes or peoples: *the Pueblo of Acoma, Pueblo traditions.*

Puerto Rico a commonwealth of the United States.

Pulaski a brand of ax used by fighters of wildfires.

pulk small sled pulled by a sled dog.

Pullman railroad car.

pulloff (n.) Use **pullout.**

pullout (n.) a place to pull off a road; preferred to **pulloff.** The verb is *pull out.*

pull-through as in an RV park.

pumpkinseed a kind of **sunfish.**

pupfish (n.)

pup tent

purchase Capitalize in the names of historical events: *the Louisiana Purchase.*

pussy willow

put in (v.), **put-in** (n.) a point of paddling access on a river. "You can *put in* at Mexican Hat." "Use the *put-in* at Mexican Hat." See **take out.**

pygmy forest

Q

Q-Tip a trademark; the generic term is *cotton swab.*

Quad Cities Davenport (Iowa) and Rock Island, Moline, and East Moline (Illinois).

quad, quadrangle when referring to USGS quadrangle or topographic maps. On second reference, *quad* is acceptable. USGS quads come in 7.5-minute series or 15-minute series. Refer to them by the names shown on the maps, in roman type: *Bluff NW quad.* The word *quad* is lowercase, a term equivalent to "map," not part of the title.

quadriceps, quads not *quadraceps.*

quahog preferred over *quahaug.*

quail, quail *quails* when referring to more than one species.

quaking aspen

quarry Capitalize only when part of a proper name. Lowercase when a descriptive term. Also see **mines.**

quarter horse

quarter hour (n.), **quarter-hour** (adj.)

quarter mile (n.), **quarter-mile** (adj.) *a quarter-mile walk.*

quasi Hyphenate compound adjectives that begin with *quasi: a quasi-professional organization, a quasi-public agency.*

Quaternary the geologic period; not *Quarternary.*

quay a wharf; not **cay** or **key,** a small island.

Quebec not *Québec.*

queen cup or **queen's cup** author preference for the common name of the plant.

queen-of-the-prairie a plant.

queue a line of people waiting.

quick draw

quicksand

Quivira a mythical city, object of Coronado's expedition in the Southwest.

quixotic (adj.) lowercase.

Quonset hut a trademark.

quotation marks See **Grammar, Punctuation, and Typography,** p. 8.

R

® the symbol for a federally registered trademark (™ means a common-law trademark). In text, there is no need to print these symbols following a capitalized trade name: "A *Gore-Tex* jacket is a must in this rainy climate." Exception: Symbols may appear on book jackets, with no space between the word and the symbol: FalconGuides®

rabbit, rabbits, kitten

rabbitbrush

rabies (s., pl.)

raccoon, raccoons, cub

racetrack

raceway a channel of water, as at a fish hatchery.

rack Two words: *roof rack, ski rack.*

radiocarbon dating or **carbon dating**

ragweed

Raid Gauloises the adventure race.

railbed

railroad Capitalize the name of a railroad; *the railroad* on second reference. Ampersands are acceptable in names, but must be used consistently. Capitalize *Amtrak* (not *AMTRAK*). Note that *transcontinental railroad* is not capitalized.

railroad bridge Capitalize the name of the railroad, but lowercase *bridge* as a descriptive term.

rain compounds *rainbow, raincoat, raindrop, rainfall, rainproof, rainstorm, rainwater,* but *rain-soaked.*

rainbow trout On second reference, *rainbows* is acceptable.

rain forest two words (one word in the names of some conservation organizations: *Rainforest Alliance*).

rain gear

Ramsar Convention or **Convention on Wetlands of International Importance** an intergovernmental treaty. Meetings held periodically since 1971. Chooses sites for the List of Wetlands of International Importance. These are *Ramsar sites.*

ranch Capitalize if the name refers to a destination for visitors, whether part of a park, a historic home, or an inn: *Lee Ranch.* Lowercase if *ranch* is merely descriptive: The *Smith ranch* lies at the foot of the Bitterroot Mountains.

rancheria Capitalize in the names of California Indian settlements: *Big Valley Rancheria, the rancheria.*

ranch hand

ranch house but **farmhouse.**

ranchland(s)

range Capitalize in the name of a mountain range: *the Front Range, the Wasatch Range,* but *the range* on second reference.

range finder preferred over *rangefinder.*

rangeland(s)

ranger station, ranger district Capitalize the full name of a ranger station: *the Kane Gulch Ranger Station,* but "Check in at the *ranger station* at Kane Gulch." Capitalize the full name of a ranger district: *Beaverhead-Deerlodge Ranger District, the ranger district, the district.*

Rapala manufacturer of lures.

rapids See **river names and features.**

rappel (v.), **rappelled** In informal usage, *rap* is acceptable.

rappel anchor

raptor any **bird of prey.**

ratcheting or **backpedaling**

ravine a narrow, deep valley.

rawhide

re- Compounds that begin with *re* are usually written as one word: *rehydrate, resole, restart.* When the second word begins with an "e," compounds may be hyphenated (should be consistent). Don't write *re-enact* on one page and *reenactment* on another. Note that the hyphen is necessary if, without a hyphen, the word would have a different meaning: *recreation* and *re-creation.*

recreation, recreational See **Appendix A: National Parks, Monuments, etc.** for form of names that include *recreation* or *recreational.* In a general sense, usually *a recreation area.* Use *recreational* as an adjective: *recreational activities.*

Recreational Equipment Inc. or **REI** no comma after *Equipment.*

recreational vehicle, RV

red Names of plants, animals, or things that begin with *red* are usually written as two words: *red cedar, red maple, red oak, red ocher, red squirrel, red tide.* Exceptions: *redfish,* and the birds *redpoll* and *redstart.*

Red Cross an international organization; the **American Red Cross** is the U.S. organization.

red-hot (adj.)

red light (n.)

red-light district

redpoint (v.) to climb a route with no falls or rests, but with practice or information about the route.

redwood(s)

refuge Capitalize when part of the full proper name: *the Bear River Migratory Bird Refuge, the Bear River refuge, the refuge.*

region Lowercase this word in phrases such as *Four Corners region, Great Lakes region.*

rein, reign *Reins* are used with horses; kings or queens *reign.*

reindeer (sing., pl.)

reinforce

Remington, Frederic (1861–1909) Western artist.

renown (n.), **renowned** (adj.) a *renowned* artist, not a *renown* artist.

repellent (adj., n.) preferred over *repellant*. Hyphenate adjective forms such as *a water-repellent coating*. Nouns are not hyphenated: *insect repellent*.

reports Titles of reports, such as military and U.S. Geological Survey reports of the nineteenth century, are treated like titles of books: capitalize and italicize.

resaca term used for certain wetlands in Texas. Also appears in proper names: *Resaca de la Palma*, a lake in Cameron County, Texas.

reservation Capitalize the proper name of an Indian reservation: *the Navajo Indian Reservation* or *the Navajo Reservation, the reservation*. If the tribe has more than one reservation, specify: *the Ramah Navajo Indian Reservation*.

resort Capitalize when part of a proper name: *Alpine Meadows Ski Resort*. But note that some ski resorts are known as *ski areas*, not *resorts*.

rest area, rest stop

restroom

reverse archaeology the practice of retracing the work of early explorers and amateur archaeologists, who collected artifacts without keeping detailed records, to try to determine the origins of objects in museum collections.

rhyolite a kind of rock; capitalized, *Rhyolite* is a Nevada ghost town.

rice field

Richter scale for measuring earthquakes.

ridable (adj.)

ridgeline

ridgetop (n., adj.)

Riel, Louis (1844–1885) leader of **Métis** rebellions in Canada. Capitalize the *Riel Rebellion.*

rifle has a rifled bore (spiral grooves in the barrel), unlike a shotgun, which has a smooth bore.

rig *S-rig, J-rig:* types of motor rigs or motorized rafts.

right-hand, left-hand (adj.)

rightmost, leftmost (adj.)

right-of-way, rights-of-way

rime/rhyme *Rime* is a coating of ice or snow; poems *rhyme.*

rimrock(s) rock or rocks on the edge of an elevated landform such as a butte or mesa.

ring-necked duck, ring-necked pheasant not *ringneck.*

ringtail preferred over *ring tail cat;* a small mammal, resembling a raccoon, found in the southwestern United States.

rio means "river" in Spanish; the *Rio Grande,* not *Rio Grande River,* which is redundant. (This redundancy is built into the administrative name of the *Rio Grande Wild and Scenic River,* however.)

riparian, riverine Both words mean "relating to riverbanks," and sometimes may be used interchangeably. *A riparian environment; riverine mammals.*

rip current, rip tide

riprap

ristra Spanish for "string"; in the Southwest, a string of chile peppers. Not italicized.

river- Many compounds beginning with *river* are written as one word: *riverbank, riverbed, riverboat, riverfront, riverside, riverway, riverweed.* Exceptions: *river basin, river bottom, river sandals.*

-river Compounds ending in *river: downriver, upriver.*

river names and features If a particular fork of a river has its own name, as in *West Fork of the Flathead River,* capitalize short forms of the name in subsequent references: *West Fork.* Also see **falls** and **narrows.** In a river guide, capitalize the commonly accepted names of river features, such as holes and rapids: "All but the most experienced rafters prefer to portage around the *Hell Hole.*"

For classification of rapids, see **class III river.**

River of Grass a name for the Florida Everglades.

River of No Return

river rafting

river runner

river valley Lowercase *valley* when it is used descriptively: *the Carmel River valley.* (*Carmel Valley* is the place.) Likewise: *Colorado River gorge.* See further discussion at **valley.**

road names See **Maps, Roads, and Directions,** p. 14.

roadbed

roadblock

road cut

roadhouse

roadless (adj.)

roadmap

roadrunner

roadside (adj., n.) a *roadside* attraction.

roadway

roadwork (n.) traffic delayed because of *roadwork.*

rock- Compounds ending in rock are generally written as one word: *rimrock, slickrock.* Capitalized, *Rock* is a trade name for a kind of nut made by Wild Country.

rock and land formations Capitalize the names of rock formations, buttes, spires, etc.: *Inscription Rock; the Mittens; Newspaper Rock.* No quotation marks around such names.

rock art a general term encompassing petroglyphs and pictographs. For further discussion of names of rock art panels, see **petroglyphs/pictographs.** No hyphen in the phrase *rock art panel.*

rock climbing (n.) two words. No hyphen

rockfall (n.)

rock hound, rockhounding

rock shelter Capitalize as part of a proper name only if the agency that manages the site does so. (The names of such sites more commonly include the word *cave*, as in *Pictograph Cave*.) *Rock shelter* is used more commonly as a descriptive term: *the Pictograph Cave rock shelter*.

rockslide (n.)

rockweed

Rocky Mountains, the Rockies Either is acceptable.

roll, Eskimo roll

roll cast

Rollerblade a trademark; use **in-line skate** instead.

roof in rock climbing, an overhang of rock.

roof rack

rooster, roosters, cockerel

rope bag

Rope Bucket a brand name of a product of A5 Adventures, now a division of the North Face. Generic term: *rope bag*.

ropelength in climbing, about 150 feet.

rope tow (n.)

rose hip or **rosehip** Either is acceptable, but be consistent.

roundhouse

round trip (n.), **round-trip** (adj.)

round-up (n.), **round up** (v.)

route numbers See **Maps, roads, and directions**, p.14.

routefinding (n.)

rowboat

RP a kind of nut, named for Roland Pauligk. Plural: *RPs*.

rucksack

ruffed grouse not *ruffled*.

rufous as in bird's names; not *Rufus,* the spelling of a man's
name.

ruins Capitalize the names of ruins in parks: *Cliff Palace* and
Spruce Tree House at Mesa Verde National Park, *Square Tower
Ruins* at Hovenweep National Monument. Also capitalize
the names of certain well-known ruins on BLM lands:
Moon House. Otherwise, lowercase as a descriptive term:
Road Canyon ruins.

runner webbing loops used in climbing.

runoff rather than *run-off;* one word preferred by most
writers in the West.

runout (n.)

RURP stands for **Realized Ultimate Reality Piton.**
Plural: *RURPs.*

Russell, A. J. (1831–1876) photographer of railroad scenes,
including the driving of the golden spike in 1869. Note the
space between the initials.

Russell, C. M. (1864–1926) Western artist. *C. M. Russell* or
Charlie Russell acceptable. The C.M. Russell Museum in Great
Falls, Montana, does not put a space between the initials.
The "M." is for "Marion."

Russian thistle more commonly known as **tumbleweed.**

RV, recreational vehicle

RV hookup(s)

S

sabal palm also called **palmetto.**

sac when referring to a plant or animal part: *egg sac, pollen sac.*

Sacagawea (1787?–1812?) not *Sacajawea.* The spelling may vary
    in titles of books and in place names, however: *Lake*
    Sakakawea, Sacajawea State Park.

sacred datura also called **jimsonweed.**

Sagebrush Rebellion

sage grouse, sage hen, sage hens, chick

saguaro not *sahuaro.*

Saguaro National Park no longer *Saguaro National Monument.*

Sahara not the *Sahara Desert,* which is redundant; *Sahara* means
    "desert."

sailboard, sailboarder, sailboarding preferred over **Windsurfer,**
    Windsurfing (which are trade names).

sailboat

Saint Spell out when part of a proper name, whether person,
    place, or thing: *Saint Joseph, Missouri; a Saint Bernard dog; Saint*
    Elmo's fire; the island of Saint Thomas. Exceptions: *Mount St. Helens,*
    Sault Ste. Marie.

saltbush

salt cedar also called **tamarisk.**

salt grass

salt lick (n.)

salt marsh

Salton Sea (California)

salt pan area where evaporated water has left a deposit of salt.

salt water (n.), **saltwater** (adj.)

San Bernardino not *San Bernadino.*

sandbag

sandbank

sandbar

sandcastle

sand dab

sand dollar

sand flea

sandhill *Sandhills of Nebraska; sandhill crane.*

sand painting, sandpainting Either is acceptable; author preference, but be consistent.

sand pipe(s) (n.) rock spires; term used at Kodachrome Basin State Park in Utah.

sandpiper

sand shark

sandstone

sandstorm

sand verbena

sand wave

Santa Ana the dry southern California wind; *Santa Anna* was the Mexican leader of the 1830s and 1840s.

Santa Fe Trail

sapodilla a kind of tree.

sapphire

sapsucker

Sasquatch or **Bigfoot**

Savannah the city in Georgia; also the *Savannah River.* For the lowercase word meaning "grasslands," *savanna* is preferred over *savannah.*

Sawatch Range in Colorado; the **Wasatch Range** is in Utah and Idaho.

sawdust

saw grass

sawmill

saw palmetto

saw-whet owl

-scape Compounds ending in *-scape* are written as one word: *cityscape, landscape, seascape.* Do not overuse to create new words.

scarp or **escarpment**

scat (n.) animal droppings.

scenic byway a byway designated under the USDA Forest Service's Scenic Byways program. A scenic byway program is also run by the Federal Highway Administration (see **National Scenic Byway**). A road can be a scenic byway under both programs. Capitalize when part of the full name: *Beartooth Highway Scenic Byway.*

scent gland (n.)

scent-mark (v.)

school When *school* refers to a school of thought, not a physical building, lowercase: *Hudson River school.* The same rule applies to schools of thought regarding skiing or climbing techniques. Also see **ski school.**

schuss (v., n.)

Schuylkill not the *Schuylkill River,* which is redundant; *kill* means "stream."

scientific names See **taxonomy.**

Scotchgard

scoter a kind of duck.

Scotts Bluff the county in Nebraska. The town is one word: *Scottsbluff.*

Scouts Use *Boy Scouts of America* or *Girl Scouts of the United States of America.* Second reference: *Boy Scouts, Girl Scouts. Scouts* is acceptable on second reference if only one of these organizations is being discussed.

scree a loose accumulation of small rocks on a slope or at the base of a cliff. Also see **talus**.

screech owl

scrimshaw

scrubland

scrub pine

scuba all lowercased. Stands for "self-contained underwater breathing apparatus."

scuba diver (n.), **scuba diving** (n.), **scuba-dive** (v.)

scull a kind of boat, or the oars used to row it; not *skull*, the bony part of the head.

sea Names of plants and animals that start with *sea* are usually written as two words: *sea anemone, sea bass, sea bream, sea cow, sea cucumber, sea grape, sea horse, sea lion, sea otter.*

sea bird

seaboard lowercase in phrases such as *Atlantic seaboard, eastern seaboard.*

sea cave

sea cliff

seacoast

seafaring (adj.)

sea floor

seafood

seagoing (adj.)

sea gull preferred over *seagull.*

sea horse

sea kayak, sea kayaking, sea kayaker no hyphen.

seal, seals, bull, cow, pup

sea level (n.)

sea lion, sea lions, bull, cow, pup

seam-seal (v.), **seam-sealed** (adj.)

seaplane also **floatplane.**

seaport

sear (v.)/**sere** (adj.) To *sear* is to burn. *Sere* means "dry."

search-and-rescue team

seashell

seashore

seasick

season Names of seasons are lowercase: *spring, summer, fall or autumn, winter.* Capitalize in bibliographic references to periodicals: *Big Sky Journal, Spring 1997.* Hyphenate *off-season* (n., adj., adv.).

seasonal/seasonable *Seasonal* means "dependent on the season": *seasonal allergies. Seasonable* means "appropriate" or "timely": *seasonable actions.*

sea stack a rock pinnacle rising out of the sea, just offshore.

sea turtle but *loggerhead turtle,* not *loggerhead sea turtle.*

sea wall preferred over *seawall.*

seaward, seawards (adv.)

seaweed

sego lily

self- Compounds with *self* are hyphenated: *self-bailing, self-belay, self-guided, self-rescue.*

semi- Compounds with *semi* are written as one word: *semiconscious, semidesert, semipalmated.* Exception: hyphenate when the second word begins with an "i."

sequoia can refer to the redwood *(Sequoia sempervirens)* or the giant sequoia *(Sequoiadendron giganteum).*

sérac

sere See note at **sear/sere.**

serviceberry not *sarvisberry.*

Seton, Ernest Thompson (1860–1946) author of *Wild Animals I Have Known* and other animal stories.

7-Eleven

Shangri-la

-shaped Use sans serif letters for *U-shaped*, *V-shaped* (as in descriptions of the shapes of valleys).

shaped skis a generic term for skis with sidecuts, as opposed to straight skis.

shard preferred over **sherd**; but *potsherd* preferred over *potshard*.

sharpshooter

Shawangunk Mountains, the Shawangunks *the Gunks* okay on second reference.

sheep (sing., pl.), ram, ewe, lamb

sheepherder or **shepherd**

sheet lightning

shell contains shot; fired by a **shotgun.** (A **cartridge** contains a bullet.)

shellfish

shell mound two words when referring to an archaeological site. May be one word in place names, however.

sheriff

Sherpa Always capitalize when referring to the people.

shin splints preferred over *shinsplints*.

ship names are always italicized, but any designation a ship may have (SS, USS) is not: SS *Minnow*, USS *Enterprise*, HMS *Titanic*, the steamboat *Yellowstone*.

Ship Rock the rock formation in northwestern New Mexico; but the town is *Shiprock*.

shoelace

shoot/chute One *shoots* rapids; a *chute* is a rapid or waterfall.

shooting *shooting star, trapshooting*.

shootout (n.) preferred over *shoot-out*.

shore bird preferred over *shorebird*.

shorefront

shoreline

shortcut

shortgrass, shortgrass prairie

shortleaf (adj.) as in *shortleaf pine.*

Shoshone not *Shoshoni* for the Indian tribe, except in the name of the *Northwestern Band of Shoshoni Nation of Utah.* Place names: *Shoshone Falls* (Idaho), *Shoshone River* (Wyoming), *Shoshoni* (town in Wyoming).

shot not interchangeable with **buckshot,** which is large-size shot.

shotgun has a smooth bore, unlike a **rifle.** A shotgun is a *smoothbore* gun. Also: a *double-barreled* shotgun.

shrew, shrews

side canyon

sidecut refers to the shape of skis.

sidehill (v.) to traverse a slope.

sidepull (n.) a climbing move.

sidesaddle

side street

side trip

sidewalk, sideways

sidewinder

Sierra *Sierra* means "mountain range" in Spanish; thus, it is the *Sierra Nevada; Sierra Nevada Mountains* is redundant. Also: *High Sierra,* not *High Sierras.*

Sierra cup

sign When referring to sign left by animals, has a plural meaning with a singular form: *sign,* not *signs.* "Other *sign* to look for: scratches, urine stain."

signage

signed (adj.) A *signed* trail is marked with signs instead of blazes or cairns.

signs *a stop sign, a yield sign.* Capitalize the words in longer signs, and do not italicize or set off in quotation marks: Watch for the *No Trespassing sign*.

siltstone

Sinagua

singletrack (n., adj.) a trail, game run, or other track with only one ribbon of walking/riding surface. Also see **doubletrack**.

sinkhole

sinter (n.) mineral deposits around hot springs and geysers. Usually used in the singular.

sipapu hole in the floor of a **kiva,** symbolic of the place of emergence.

site/sight A *site* is a place: *a historic site*. A *sight* is something seen: *a rare sight*. (To *cite* is to quote or refer to something.)

sit-on-top (n.) a kayak not requiring the use of a spray skirt.

Sitting Bull (1831?–1890) the Sioux leader.

six-gun, six-shooter

Six Nations the Iroquois Confederacy.

six-pack

sizable preferred over *sizeable*.

skarn a kind of rock.

skate See **ice skate, in-line skate.**

skateboard

skate-ski (v.)

skeg part of a boat.

ski Compound nouns beginning with *ski* are usually written as two words: *ski boot, ski jump, ski lift, ski lodge, ski patrol, ski pole, ski rack, ski tow*. Exception: *skiwear*.

Ski-Doo a brand of snowmobile.

skijoring (n.) skiing while being pulled by a horse, a vehicle, or (in the most common use of the term today) a sled dog. Not *ski-joring*.

skillful not *skilful*.

skin-dive, skin diver, skin diving

skinny-dip, skinny-dipping

Skin-So-Soft Avon product thought by some to work as an insect repellent.

skintight (adj.)

ski patrol Capitalize the name of the organization, the *National Ski Patrol*, and the names of ski patrols associated with individual ski areas. Note that such ski patrols do not necessarily share the name of their ski area: *Skyline Ski Patrol* at Heavenly Ski Resort.
The National Ski Patrol is the U.S. organization. The Canadian Ski Patrol System is the equivalent organization in Canada.

ski resorts, ski schools Capitalize *ski resort* when commonly used as part of the name: *Alpine Meadows Ski Resort.* (The name of the corporation that owns the resort may be completely different.) Note that some resorts are called *ski areas*, not *ski resorts*. Also capitalize *ski school* when used with the name of the resort: the *Alpine Meadows Ski School*, but *the ski school at Alpine Meadows.*

ski runs and areas Follow local usage in capitalizing: *the West Bowl* at Lake Louise.

skunk, skunks, kitten

skunk cabbage

skydive (v.), **skydiver, skydiving**

slalom

slay, sleigh To *slay* is to kill. A *sleigh* is a horse-drawn sled.

sled dog

sleeping bag

sleeping car

sleigh See note at **slay/sleigh.**

slew/slough *Slew* is the past tense of **slay**, to kill. A *slew* (n.) is a large number: *a slew of visitors.* A *slough* is a marsh: *Elkhorn Slough.*

slickrock (n., adj.) rock formations eroded smooth and round. Large expanses of such formations are found throughout the Southwest.

Slickrock Trail (Moab, Utah)

slot canyon

slough See note at **slew/slough.**

smallmouth one word when referring to the fish: *smallmouth bass.*

smear (v.) to use the friction of shoe against rock in climbing.

Smithsonian Institution not *Smithsonian Institute.*

smokejumper

Smokey Bear not *Smokey the Bear.* This is a variant spelling of "smoky" for this name only.

smoky (adj.) Use this spelling for everything except **Smokey Bear.**

smoothbore (adj.)

s'mores

snag a dead tree where birds may nest.

snorkel, snorkeling

snow Compounds beginning with *snow* that are written as one word: *snowball, snowbank, snowbird, snowbound, snowdrift, snowfall, snowfield, snowflake, snowman, snowmelt, snowmobile, snowpack, snow-plow, snowshoes, snowstorm.* Compounds written as two words: *snow blower, snow cave, snow fence, snow goose, snow pellet(s), snow tire.*

snow-blind (adj.), **snow blindness** (n.)

snowboard

snowcapped (adj.)

snowcat generic term for a tracked snow vehicle. *Tucker Sno-Cat* is a maker of such vehicles.

snowcoach a passenger snow bus. Lowercase. Capitalized, *SnoCoach* or *Snocoach* are spellings used by Brewster, the Canadian tour company.

snow line the point of elevation in alpine regions where snow can first be found.

snowmachine term often used in Alaska for *snowmobile.* Riders are *snowmachiners.*

snowmaking

snowshoe (n., v.), **snowshoeing**

snow-white (adj.)

snowy (adj.) as in *snowy egret, snowy owl.*

sockeye salmon, sockeyes

Soil Conservation Service now called the Natural Resources Conservation Service (NRCS).

solar shower used as a generic term. Capitalize the brand name, **Sun Shower.**

solo climbing climbing alone, or without a rope or other gear. "Free soloing" is solo climbing without ropes; "roped soloing" is solo climbing with ropes.

solstice Lowercase: *summer solstice, winter solstice.*

-some Compounds ending in *-some* and meaning a group of people are written as one word: *twosome, threesome,* and so on.

sonar Lowercase; stands for "sound navigation and ranging."

songbird

sopaipilla a deep-fried New Mexican pastry.

sorghum

sotol, sotol grasslands

Soufrière Capitalize in the names of several volcanoes in the Caribbean.

south, southern Lowercase when *south* is a direction: Head *south* for one mile. Capitalize when referring to the region, *the South.* Capitalize *southern* according to common usage in the names of some regions: *Southern California,* but *southern Oregon.* Also capitalize *southern* when it is part of the name of an Indian tribe, whether the official name of a tribe today or a commonly accepted historical designation: *the Southern Utes.* For states included in the South, see **United States.**

south-central not *southcentral;* but *southwest, southeast.*

Southeast synonymous with the Census Bureau's **South Atlantic.**

Southern Hemisphere

southernmost

South Pole but *the pole, polar.*

southwest Capitalize when naming the region: *the Southwest,* but *the southwestern United States.* The Southwest includes Nevada, Utah, Arizona, New Mexico, western Texas, and parts of Southern California.

spaghetti Western

spandex lowercase; not a trademark.

Spanish rubber, sticky rubber used for the soles of climbing shoes.

spartan lowercase generally: *a spartan cabin.* Capitalize only when referring to Sparta, the city in ancient Greece.

species names See **genus;** also see **taxonomy.**

species of special concern an administrative designation. Lowercase: The Steller sea lion is an Alaska *species of special concern.*

Spectra trademark for fiber used in climbing rope and cord.

spelunker, spelunking *caver, caving* preferred unless referring to scientific exploration. The scientific study of caverns and related features is *speleology.*

SPF short for sun protection factor, referring to the strength of sunscreen products. Use with a numeral: *SPF 30.*

spiderweb

spindrift seafoam; also used to refer to blowing snow.

split second (n.)

spoil banks, spoil island land forms created by dredging.

sport Compound verbs with *sport* are generally written as two words: *sport climbing, sport fishing.*

sport-utility vehicle, SUV

spotting scope

spray skirt

spring-fed (adj.)

springtime

spud in ice fishing, tool used to chop a hole in the ice.

spur (n.) a side road or trail that splits off from the main route. Not *spur road* or *spur trail*.

squaw an offensive term. Use only in direct quotations, as in historical references, or in proper names: *Squaw Valley*. (Some such place names have been renamed recently.) See **Nondiscriminatory Language,** p. 23.

squeeze chimney

stagecoach

Staked Plains also known as the **Llano Estacado.**

stalactite, stalagmite Stalactites hang from the ceiling, stalagmites rise from the ground.

standard time See **time zones.**

starboard, port *Starboard* is the right-hand side of the ship, as you face forward; *port* is the left-hand side.

starfish

stargaze, stargazing

stars Names of **constellations** are capitalized: *the Big Dipper, Orion.*

state Usually lowercase the word *state,* as in *the state of Montana.* Exceptions: *Washington State* and *New York State* if necessary to distinguish from Washington, D.C., and New York City. Also see **commonwealth.**

state birds, flowers, and other symbols Such terms are lowercase, as descriptive terms: The bitterroot is the *state flower* of Montana.

state line two words when referring to the border between states, but one word for the Nevada town, *Stateline.*

state nicknames Capitalize, and do not set off with quotation marks: Arizona is known as the *Grand Canyon State.*

statewide (adj.)

station Capitalize when part of a proper name: *Grand Central Station.* Also capitalize *station* or *depot* following the name of a town, if the station is commonly known by that name (even though the formal name may differ): *the Ketchum Depot.* Lowercase when referring to a TV or radio station.

stationary (adj.)/**stationery** (n.) *Stationary* means "standing still." *Stationery* is writing paper.

staysail

Stealth rubber a trademark for sticky rubber used on climbing shoes.

steamboat

steelhead

steeplechase

Steller a name that appears in several common names of animals: *Steller sea lion, Steller's jay.* Not *stellar,* meaning "of the stars" or "outstanding."

stem (v.) to span with the legs in climbing.

steppe a plain, as in Siberia; not a *step,* which one takes in walking.

steppingstone

Sterno

Stetson brand name for a kind of hat.

Sticht plate a kind of belay plate.

still water (n.), **still-water** (adj.)

stingray

stock tank

-stone Compounds ending in *stone* are generally written as one word: *gemstone, mudstone, sandstone, siltstone.* Capitalize *Stone,* brand name of a product made by Wild Country.

Stone Age

stonefly

Stone sheep

stopover (n.)

Stopper a brand of chock. Should be capitalized, although it is often seen lowercase.

stopwatch

-storm Compounds ending in *storm* are generally written as one word: *hailstorm, rainstorm, snowstorm*, but *ice storm*.

Stowe a ski area in Vermont, not *Stow*.

strait, straits In proper names, it is usually singular: *Bering Strait, Strait of Gibraltar*, but *Straits of Mackinac*. Capitalize when part of a proper name, otherwise lowercase: *the strait*.

stratum, strata

-stream In compounds: *downstream, upstream*.

stream bank

streambed

stream bottom

streamside

streetlight

strip mine (n.), **strip-mine** (v.)

stuff sack

Styrofoam a trademark.

sub- Compounds beginning with *sub* are written as one word: *subalpine, subbasement, subculture, subspecies, subsurface, subzero*.

such as, like When giving examples, *such as* and *like* are interchangeable.

sugar Names of plants that start with *sugar* are usually written as two words: *sugar beet, sugar cane, sugar maple, sugar pine*. Exception: in names of mountains or hills, often one word: *Sugarloaf*.

suit *wetsuit, drysuit*.

sulfur not *sulphur*, except often in place names: *sulfur hot springs*, but *White Sulphur Springs* (Montana and West Virginia).

Summer Olympics Also see **Olympics.**

sun Like the earth and the moon, capitalize only *sun* in the context of other heavenly bodies.

sun Compounds beginning with *sun* are generally written as one word: *sunbaked, sunbathe, sunbeam, sunburn, sundown, sunglasses, sunlight, sunrise, sunroof, sunset, sunshine, sunstroke, suntan, sunup.* Exceptions: *sun block, sun deck.*

sunbather but **sun worshiper**

Sunbelt

sun block but *sunscreen.*

sun crust a kind of snow surface.

sun dance two words, lowercase, for the American Indian dance. One word, *Sundance,* for the film festival in Utah.

sundew the plant; may be two words in some place names.

sunfish (sing., pl.)

sun protection factor, SPF

sunscreen but **sun block.**

Sun Shower a brand name. Generic term: *solar shower.*

Superfund a program of the Environmental Protection Agency that cleans up hazardous waste sites: *a Superfund site.*

super-sidecut skis a generic term.

Supplex a trademark.

surefooted

surfbird

surfboard

survey Capitalize when part of the name of a government unit or a historical expedition: *the Hayden Survey, the King Survey, the U.S. Geological Survey.*

Suwannee River

swami

swami belt a primitive climbing harness.

swamp boat

swampland

swan, swans, cygnet

Sweet Grass County, Sweet Grass Hills (Montana)

Sweetwater River, Sweetwater County (Wyoming)

Swiftcurrent Lodge, Swiftcurrent Mountain in Glacier
National Park; but *Swift Current*, the town in Saskatchewan.

swimmer's itch

swimming hole

swimming pool

swimsuit but **bathing suit**

Swiss Army knife

switchback (n.) The zigzag of a trail up a steep slope to ease
the gradient of the climb. Sometimes used as a verb
meaning to move in a zigzag pattern: "We *switchbacked* up
the mountain."

swordfish

Synchilla a trademark of Patagonia.

syncline

system Capitalize when part of an organizational name, such
as *the National Park System, the Wild and Scenic Rivers System, the
Alaska State Park System.* Lowercase when referring to a natural
area: *the Apalachee Bay system.*

T

tableland A plateau or (depending on regional usage) a **mesa**.

taiga area of forest just south of the tundra. *Taiga forest* redundant.

-tailed Hyphenate in compounds in animal names: *white-tailed deer*, but *whitetail*.

tailgate not *tailgait*.

tailwind

takeoff (n.), **take off** (v.)

take out (v.), **take-out** (n.) a point of paddling access. See **put in**.

tallgrass, tallgrass prairie

talus an accumulation of broken cliff fragments on the slope of a mountain or at the base of a cliff. Such fragments can range in size from footballs to office furniture. Accumulations of larger rocks generally are called *boulder fields;* accumulations of smaller rocks are called *scree.*

Tamalpais, Mount a peak in Marin County, California. Not *Tamalpias.*

tamarack/tamarisk *Tamarack* is a deciduous larch; *tamarisk* is a shrub also known as **salt cedar.**

taproot

tarpon a kind of fish.

taxonomy Scientific names are best dealt with on a case-by-case basis. Occasionally names are revised, as species are reclassified as subspecies or vice versa. Use the *American Heritage Dictionary* and current editions of Audubon field guides and taxonomic publications to determine the most appropriate spelling of the Latin name of a plant or animal.

The following general rules apply: In a name of the form *Canis lupus* (gray wolf), the first word is the genus name, the second is the species name. The genus name is capitalized; the species name is lowercase. Both are italicized.

Genus and species names can be the same: *Alces alces* (moose). Subspecies names, when used, follow species names and also are italicized: *Alces alces shirasi*. In scientific names, the species name is always lowercase, even when derived from a person's name or from a former genus: *Lesquerella gordoni*. However, when a subspecies is distinguished by the discoverer's name, that name is not italicized: *Bufo woodhousei* Woodhouse.

On first reference, give the complete genus and species name. On second reference, the genus name can be abbreviated: *C. lupus*. Additional designations such as *sp.* or *var.* are in roman type following the name. A lowercase *sp.* following a genus name indicates that the species is not specified: *Arbutus* sp. (a madrone of some kind). A lowercase *var.* following a genus and species name indicates a variety: *Arbutus menziesii* var.

Larger divisions than genus, such as class, order, and family, are capitalized and set in roman type: Mustelidae family (weasels and skunks). Note that *family* is lowercase. Lowercase and roman type for the English version of a Latin family name: mustelids.

Common names are not capitalized, unless a proper name is part of the common name: *gray wolf, mule deer, Townsend's pocket gopher*.

Taylor Grazing Act of 1934

T-bar

TCU abbreviation for a **Three Cam Unit**. Plural: *TCUs*.

team names Capitalize: *U.S. Ski Team*, but *the ski team* on second reference.

Technicolor a trademark.

Teflon a trademark.

telemark turn (n.) lowercase. On second reference, the short form *tele-turn* is okay.

téléphérique a kind of European ski lift; italicize; but *gondola* or *cable car* preferred.

telephone numbers Use the form *406-442-6597*. For toll-free numbers: *800-582-2665*. Always include the area code.

television and radio programs Italicize the title of a continuing series: *Bay Area Backroads*. Capitalize and set off in quotation marks, but do not italicize, the title of an individual episode: "Winning Over Wolf Reintroduction Opponents," an episode of National Public Radio's *Living on Earth* series.

temblor an earthquake. Not *tremblor*.

temperature In text, use the abbreviation *F* (no period) instead of the word *Fahrenheit: 57 degrees F.* To give a range of temperatures: *The temperature can drop 15 to 20 degrees after sundown.* To give negative temperatures: *-15 degrees F* or *15 below zero*, not *minus 15*. Spell out the word *zero:* In January, *below-zero* temperatures are not unusual.

In cookbooks and hot springs guides, use the degree symbol: *Bake at 375° for 3 hours.* Fahrenheit temperatures are assumed.

Tenaya Canyon in Yosemite National Park. When referring to a natural rock basin, use the spelling **tinaja**.

tendinitis not *tendonitis*, but **tendon**.

tent site but **campsite**.

Tenth Mountain Division Hut System *a Tenth Mountain Division ski hut*.

tepee not *tipi* or *teepee*.

terrain/terrane *Terrain* is land; *terrane* is a geological term meaning an area dominated by a particular kind of rock.

territory Lowercase before a proper name, but capitalized after: *the territory of Oklahoma*, but *Oklahoma Territory*.

testpiece (n.)

that, which, who See **Grammar, Punctuation and Typography**, p. 8.

the not usually capitalized before a place name, with a few exceptions: *The Dalles* (Oregon), but *the Dalles region.* Before the name of an organization, *the* may be capitalized as part of the name: *The Nature Conservancy.* Follow the preference of the organization. See **Appendix E: Outdoor clubs and organizations.**

Therm-a-Rest a brand of camping pad.

Thermos still a trademark, but often used lowercase and generally, rather than the generic term *vacuum bottle.*

thin crack in rock climbing, a crack up to 1.25 inches wide.

thin face in rock climbing, a rock face with only small holds.

Thinsulate trademark for a kind of insulation.

Thomas Gilcrease Institute of American History and Art in Tulsa, Oklahoma.

Thompson, David (1770–1857) Canadian mapmaker and explorer.

Thoreau, Henry David (1817–1862) author of *Walden* and *A Week on the Concord and Merrimack Rivers.*

threatened and endangered species See **endangered species.**

Three Cam Unit or **TCU** not *3CU.*

three-pin binding but the binding has *three pins.*

through-hiking, through-hikers on the Appalachian Trail.

thunder- Compounds beginning with *thunder* are generally written as one word: *thunderbolt* (but *lightning bolt*), *thunderclap, thundercloud, thunderhead, thundershower, thunderstorm.*

tidal wave The correct term for a wave caused by an earthquake is **tsunami.**

tide *high tide, low tide, red tide.*

tidelands

tidepool

tide table

tidewater Capitalized, *Tidewater* appears in many Virginia place names.

tiedown (n.)

tie in (v.), **tie-in** (n., adj.) *Tie in* to the rope; a *tie-in* point; check your *tie-in.*

till (n.) in a geological context, sediment from a glacier.

timberland

timberline the point of altitude in mountainous regions above which trees do not grow (see **tree line**).

-time Compounds ending in *time,* referring to seasons or times of day, are written as one word: *springtime, daytime, nighttime.*

time 6 A.M. (not 6:00 and not a.m. or am). 5:30 P.M. "Hours are from 1 to 4:30 P.M." A.M. and P.M. should be set in small caps, with no space between the elements.
If referring generally to a half-hour or quarter-hour, spell out: "We arrived *around half past four,*" not *"around 4:30."* Use numerals if the precise time is important, as in giving hours of operation.

time-lapse (adj.)

time zones Capitalize only the words that are proper nouns: *Pacific daylight time, mountain standard time.* Note that the Navajo Reservation in Arizona observes daylight-saving time, while the rest of Arizona does not. This is so that the reservation observes the same time as other parts of the reservation, which are in New Mexico and Utah.

tinaja a natural rock basin where water collects. But **Tenaya Canyon** in Yosemite National Park.

T intersection

tip-up (n.) used to hold a line in ice fishing.

Tocqueville, Alexis de (1805–1859) author of *Democracy in America.*

toehold (n.)

tollbooth

toll bridge

tomb Capitalize when part of a proper name: *Grant's Tomb, Tomb of the Unknown Soldier* or *Tomb of the Unknowns.*

tombolo sandbar between island and mainland or between two islands: *a tombolo beach.*

Tony Accetta brand of lures.

topographic map not *topographical map*; on second reference, *topo* or *topo map* acceptable. U.S. Geological Survey topos come in 7.5-minute and 15-minute series. Also see **quadrangle**.

Topographical Engineers See Corps of Topographical Engineers.

top out (v.) to emerge at the top of a cliff upon completion of a rock climb.

toprope (n., v.)

topwater (adj.)

tornado, tornadoes

torque, torqued, torquing

torreya lowercase for the kind of tree.

tortoise(s)

tortuous/torturous *Tortuous* means "twisting": a *tortuous* mountain road. *Torturous* means "relating to torture": a *torturous* experience.

total eclipse

totem pole

touring canoe, touring kayak

toward (prep.) not *towards.*

towhee If necessary to hyphenate, break "tow-hee."

-town Compounds ending in *town* that are written as two words: *ghost town, mining town.* One word: *boomtown, shantytown.*

township a unit of survey; further divided into sections. Follows the same rule as **territory**: lowercase before a name, capitalize after. Place names in Maine sometimes take the form *Township 6 North of Weld.*

townsite an area set aside through legal action for the development of a human settlement, surveyed and with streets laid out. Also, this usage slightly extended to refer to towns now uninhabited which have not expanded beyond their original townsites (as in a deserted mining boomtown of the old West). Outside North America, the term refers simply to the site occupied by a town.

towpath next to a canal.

towtruck

track stand (v.) to balance a bike in one place.

trackway one word when referring to dinosaur tracks.

trademarks are capitalized: *Gore-Tex*. Do not set in all caps. Not necessary to include ™ or ® in text.

trade wind

trading post Capitalize when part of a proper name: *Hubbell Trading Post*, but *the trading post; Hatch Trading Post*, but *the trading post at Hatch.*

trail biker one who rides a motorcycle equipped for off-road riding (see **mountain biker**).

trailhead Do not capitalize except at the beginning of a sentence or as part of a proper name: *Dog Canyon Trailhead.*

trail mix

trail names For numbered trails, do not use the # symbol or the abbreviation *No.* before the number: *Trail 62.* Capitalize the names of trails: *Bear Creek Trail, the Appalachian Trail.* When several trails or trailheads are mentioned in a description of a hike, to avoid confusion, clearly state each trail name or number on each reference. When only one trail is being discussed, *the trail* is okay on second reference.
Trail names are also capitalized in historic references and in road names: *Burr Trail, Oregon Trail, Trail of Tears.*

trail rider not *backcountry horseman* unless mentioning the name of an organization in which the latter term appears.

trail running (n.) no hyphen.

trains See **railroads.**

Trango Pyramid trade name for a belay device.

transatlantic

Trans-Canada Highway

transceiver

transcontinental railroad lowercase.

traveler, traveled, traveling not *traveller, travelled, travelling*.

traveler's check(s) American Express spells it *Travelers Cheques*, however.

travelogue not *travelog*.

traverse (n., v.) referring to moving across, not up or down, a slope or cliff.

travois (sing., pl.)

tread (n.) the surface of a mountain bike trail.

treaty Capitalize the formal name of a treaty: *Fort Laramie Treaty of 1851*, but *the treaty of 1851*. Lowercase when referred to by the name of a tribe or author's name: *the Stevens treaty, the Navajo treaty*.

tree line the northernmost or southernmost latitude beyond which trees do not grow (see **timberline**).

tree names As with nicknames of mountains, capitalize tree nicknames (often given to very large or old trees), but do not set off by quotation marks: *the giant sequoia, General Sherman*. Also see **common names** and **taxonomy**.

tree-lined (adj.)

tree of life (n.)

tree-ring dating

trek, trekker, trekking

trench For ocean trenches, follow the same rule as for **canyons,** and capitalize: *the Mariana Trench*, but *the trench*.

triathlon not *triathalon*.

tribal park Capitalize this term when it is part of the formal name of a park: *Monument Valley Tribal Park, Ute Mountain Tribal Park*. Lowercase as a descriptive term when used alone: *The Four Corners Monument is a Navajo tribal park*.

tribe Capitalize the word *tribe* if that is how the tribe is known as an administrative entity: *the Hopi Tribe.* Other tribes are known in other ways: *Navajo Nation; the Pueblo of San Ildefonso; Turtle Mountain Band of Chippewa Indians of North Dakota; Alturas Indian Rancheria.* In such cases, *tribe* is lowercase: *the Navajo tribe.* Also see **Appendix B: Indian tribes.**

Tri-Cam a brand name of Lowe.

Tri-Cities Kennewick, Pasco, and Richland (Washington).

Trinity Site at the White Sands Missile Range.

tripod

troad(s) (n.) a coinage meaning a cross between a trail and a road. Use the term **doubletrack** instead.

troop/troupe A *troop* is any group, or a military unit. A *troupe* is a group of performers.

tropic of Cancer, tropic of Capricorn, the tropics, tropical

tropicbird

trout (sing., pl.)

T-shirt Always capitalize the *T.* Not *tee shirt.*

tsunami

tube chock a kind of nut used in climbing.

tufa/tuff *Tufa* refers to rock deposits formed in water: the *tufa* spires of Mono Lake. *Tuff* is rock made of volcanic ash.

tugboat

tules are bulrushes; in California, *tule* also refers to marshy land, hence *tule elk, tule fog.* One word for the town in Siskiyou County, *Tulelake.*

tulip tree

tumbleweed also called **Russian thistle.**

tundra in the Arctic, the area between the **tree line** and the polar icecap.

tunnel Capitalize when part of a proper name: *the Wawona Tunnel, the tunnel.* Lowercase when used as a descriptive term: *the Zion–Mount Carmel Highway tunnels.*

Tuolumne in several place names in Yosemite National Park.

tupelo

turkey, turkeys, tom, hen, poult

turnaround (n.), **turn around** (v.)

Turner, Frederick Jackson (1861–1932) American historian who argued the importance of the frontier.

turnoff (n.), **turn off** (v.)

turnpike Capitalize when part of a proper name; *the turnpike* on second reference.

turquoise

Twentynine Palms no hyphen in the name of the town just outside Joshua Tree National Park. Not *29 Palms*.

Twin Cities Minneapolis and Saint Paul, Minnesota.

two-way radio

type, kind may be used interchangeably. Use *species*, however, when the context calls for a precise, scientific term. Thus, in a hiking guidebook, "you may see several *kinds* of hawk" or "you may see several *types* of hawk"—either is appropriate. In a field guide or wildlife viewing guide: "This marsh is habitat for many bird *species*."

U

UFO, UFOs

UIAA, Union Internationale des Associations d'Alpinisme

Uinta, Uintah *Uinta* for the river and national forest in Utah, and for the mountains in Utah and Wyoming; also a county in Wyoming. *Uintah County*, in Utah; *Uintah and Ouray Indian Reservation; Uintah Mountain Club.*

U-lock

ultralight (adj.)

un- Compounds with the prefix *un* are written as one word: *unclip, unmatched, unnatural, unnerving, unsurpassed.* Exception: hyphenate when the second word is a proper noun: *un-American.*

Uncompahgre National Forest, Peak, Plateau

under- Compounds beginning with *under* are usually written as one word: *undercling, undersea, understory, undertow, underwater.*

Underground Railroad

underwater (adj., adv.)

under way (adv., adj.)

UNESCO is the **United Nations Educational, Scientific and Cultural Organization.**

Union Pacific Railroad

Union Internationale des Associations d'Alpinisme, UIAA

unique means the only such thing. Should be used sparingly; phrases like "very unique" should not be used at all. Instead, use *unusual, rare, distinctive,* or some other such word that conveys a less than absolute meaning.

unit Capitalize units of parks: the *Needles District* of
Canyonlands National Park.

United States Always spell out when used as a noun; use *U.S.*
(no space between the elements) only as an adjective.

When giving a road name, write *U.S. Highway 12*, but *US 12*.

The Census Bureau divides the states into the following
regions and divisions:

Northeast includes:

New England: Maine, New Hampshire, Vermont,
Massachusetts, Rhode Island, Connecticut.

Mid-Atlantic: New York, New Jersey, Pennsylvania.

Midwest includes:

East North Central: Ohio, Indiana, Illinois, Michigan,
Wisconsin.

West North Central: Minnesota, Iowa, Missouri, North
Dakota, South Dakota, Nebraska, Kansas.

South includes:

South Atlantic: Delaware, Maryland, District of Columbia,
Virginia, West Virginia, North Carolina, South Carolina,
Georgia, Florida.

East South Central: Kentucky, Tennessee, Alabama,
Mississippi.

West South Central: Arkansas, Louisiana, Oklahoma, Texas.

West includes:

Mountain: Montana, Idaho, Wyoming, Colorado, New
Mexico, Arizona, Utah, Nevada.

Pacific: Washington, Oregon, California, Alaska, Hawaii.

Note that some terms, such as **Great Plains, Midwest,
Pacific Northwest,** and **Southwest,** are used more commonly
than some of these Census Bureau divisions.

Unknown Soldier, Tomb of the or **Tomb of the
Unknowns** *the tomb* on second reference.

up When *up* is part of a verb, do not hyphenate: *back up, beef
up, follow up, give up.* The adjective form may be one word, as

in *a backup plan.* Otherwise hyphenate: *a follow-up story.*

up- When *up* is used as a prefix (whether an adjective or an
adverb), write as one word: *upcurrent, updraft, uphill, upriver,
upstate, upstream.*

upper Capitalize when considered part of a proper name:
Upper Peninsula (Michigan), *Upper Waterton Lake.* Also see
falls and **lakes.** Also capitalize *upper* when it is part of
the formal name of an Indian tribe: *Upper Skagit Indian
Tribe of Washington.*

Upper Midwest usually synonymous with the **Great Lakes
states.**

upside down (adv.), **upside-down** (adj.)

upstate Lowercase this word in phrases such as *upstate New York.*

U.S. Board on Geographic Names the ultimate authority
on geographic names in the United States. The equivalent
board in Canada is the Canadian Permanent Committee
on Geographical Names. See discussion in **Names and
Capitalization,** p. 16, and **Nondiscriminatory Language,**
p. 23.

USDA abbreviation for United States Department of
Agriculture.

USDA Forest Service not *U.S. Forest Service.* Use arabic
numerals when referring to regional divisions: *Region 1.*

use/utilize These words are not interchangeable. *Utilize* means
"to put to use": "The injured hiker survived by *utilizing* his
guidebook as a splint." In almost all cases, however, *use* is
preferred as shorter and less pretentious in tone.

use *day use area, limited use permit.*

user-night (n.) a park management term.

U-shaped valley Use a sans serif **U.**

Utahn not *Utahan,* when referring to a resident of Utah.

utopia Lowercase in general references; *Utopia* only when
referring to the place in the book by Sir Thomas More.

U-turn

UV rays short for ultraviolet rays.

V

vacuum bottle generic term for the brand name **Thermos** (but *thermos*, lowercase, has also become acceptable as a generic term).

vade mecum a guidebook; Latin, but no need to italicize.

valley Capitalize when part of a proper name: *Death Valley, Valley of Fire*. If in doubt, check whether the valley is named on the USGS map for that area.

Lowercase *valley* when used as a descriptive term following a complete proper name: *the Missouri River valley*. Guideline: Like the word "coast," *valley* can be capitalized when referring to a settled region, lowercase when referring to a geographical area. Thus, birds of the *Rio Grande valley*, but residents of the *Rio Grande Valley*. (In such cases, larger, more populated regions are more likely to have *valley* capitalized.) Use a sans serif font for the letter in the terms *U-shaped* or *V-shaped valley*.

Vaseline a trademark; the generic term is *petroleum jelly*.

vehicles Makes of vehicles are capitalized, but generic terms like *truck* are not: *a Jeep Cherokee, a Ford truck*. When stating the year: *a 1996 Jeep Cherokee* or, informally, *a '96 Cherokee*.

Velcro a trademark, so capitalize.

veldt in Africa, a plain.

veranda or **verandah** either is okay; author preference, but should be consistent.

verbs In books, generally use the present tense when quoting speakers: *"This is one of my favorite hikes," Ranger Bob says*.

verdant/vernal *Verdant* means "green"; *vernal* refers to spring.

verglas a thin layer of ice on rock.

vermilion preferred over *vermillion,* but place names vary: *Vermilion Cliffs* in Arizona, *Vermilion Peak* in Colorado; *Vermillion Bluffs* and *Vermillion Creek* in Colorado, and *Vermillion,* South Dakota (the town). Use the spelling on USGS maps.

vernal See usage note at **verdant.** A *vernal pool* is seasonal.

VIA Rail Canada Inc. Canada's passenger railway.

Vibram a trade name, so capitalize.

viga(s) projecting roof beams, as in pueblo-style architecture.

vision quest

visitor center not *visitors center* or *visitor's center* (but in a national park, follow the park's usage). Capitalize when part of a proper name: *Needles Visitor Center.*

VISTA Volunteers in Service to America.

V-neck

volcano, volcanoes as in *Hawaii Volcanoes National Park.*

vole, voles

Volunteers in Parks (VIP) Capitalize references to the volunteer program found in many parks.

Voyage of Discovery Capitalize when referring to the **Lewis and Clark Expedition,** also known as the **Corps of Discovery.**

voyageur(s)

W

walkie-talkie lowercase.

walk-in (adj.) as in *a walk-in campsite.*

Wallace, Alfred Russel (1823–1913) British naturalist and theorist of evolution; not *Russell.*

walleye

Wallnut a brand of nut.

Wallowa the lake, mountains, national forest, and river in Oregon.

Wal-Mart

walrus (sing., pl.), **bull, cow, calf**

Walton, Izaak (1593–1683) author of *The Compleat Angler.*

wand(s) in mountaineering, stakes used to mark a route: *a wanded track.*

want list (n.) the list of birds a birder wants to see. No hyphen.

wapiti, wapitis See **elk.**

warm-blooded (adj.)

warmwater or **warm-water** (adj.), **warm water** (n.) Use *warmwater* (adj.) when contrasting a habitat to **coldwater** conditions, as for fishing. Hyphenate *warm-water* (adj.) when simply describing the temperature: *These warm-water conditions are great for sea kayaking.*

Wasatch Front

Wasatch Range in Utah and Idaho; **Sawatch Range** in Colorado.

wash Capitalize when part of a proper name: *Courthouse Wash,*

but *the wash* on second reference. Check to see whether the
wash is named on the USGS map for that area.

washboard (adj.) describes poorly graded dirt roads; after heavy
vehicle traffic, they become corrugated and extremely bumpy.

wastewater (n.) May appear as two words in some proper
names, as of wastewater treatment plants.

Watchable Wildlife a registered trademark of Falcon.

water- Some compounds beginning with *water* that are written
as one word: *waterborne, waterbus, watercolor, watercourse, watercraft,
waterfall, waterfront, waterlogged, waterproof, watershed, waterside, waterspout, waterway.* Compounds that are two words: *water lily, water
moccasin, water wheel, water wings.*

water bar a log or other barrier placed on a trail to prevent
erosion.

water bird but **waterfowl.**

waterfalls See **falls.**

water gap a gap in a mountain ridge through which a stream
runs. Capitalize when part of a proper name: *Delaware Water
Gap.* Also see **wind gap.**

water hole/watering hole A *water hole* is where animals drink;
a *watering hole* is a bar or saloon.

Waterpocket Fold formation included in Capitol Reef National
Park.

water-repellent (adj.)

water-resistant (adj.)

water ski (n.), **water-ski** (v.), **water-skier** (n.), **waterskiing** (n.)

water snake

water sports

waterspout

water table

water tower

Watkins, Carleton E. (1829–1916) photographer known for
photographs of Yosemite.

wattle and daub (n.) a building constructed of *wattle and daub; wattle-and-daub* construction.

wave *big wave, sand wave, tidal wave.*

WaveRunner a brand of personal watercraft made by Yamaha.

wave ski lowercase.

weakfish

-weap, -weep Spellings of place names in the Southwest vary. *Hovenweep National Monument; Toroweap Point* at the Grand Canyon, but *Tuweep.* Check the spelling on USGS maps.

weasel, weasels

Weather Bureau a former name; now called the **National Weather Service.**

website lowercase; but capitalize *World Wide Web.*
Web addresses: Leave out the *http* at the beginning; lowercase all letters; don't end in a slash; may end in *html* or *htm.* Cannot end in *htmi* (an easy misprint for *html*). Put a final period if the address falls at the end of a sentence: *Look up national park information at www.nps.gov/index.html.*

-weed Compounds ending in *weed* are generally written as one word: *ragweed, seaweed, tumbleweed.*

weedbed

weed guard

weedless spoon a kind of lure.

well Compounds with *well* are hyphenated before the noun, but not after: *Those animals are well camouflaged,* but *well-camouflaged animals are hard to see.*

well-being (n.)

west, western Always lowercase when *west* and *western* are used as directions or descriptive terms: The wind was coming from the *west.* Her hobby is painting *western* wildflowers.
Capitalize when *west* is used as part of the name of a region (whether actual or a state of mind): *the West, the West Coast, the Wild West, the Far West.*

Capitalize *western* when referring to arts or culture: John

Wayne's *Western* films; Charlie Russell, the *Western* artist. That said, it must be admitted that, more so than *east, north,* or *south, west* can be difficult to categorize as a direction or a region, a lowercase descriptive term or a capitalized cultural term. A few guidelines: Birds fly *south* for the winter (not *South*); likewise, "Go *west,* young man." She drove *west* until sunset (*west* tells what direction she drove in). They went *West* in 1849, hoping to strike it rich (*West* names the region they went to).

The terms *out west* and *back east* fall somewhere between stating a direction of travel and naming a region. In some contexts, you may prefer to lowercase these terms, as you would lowercase "outback" or "backcountry": They take their vacation *out west* every year. In other contexts, you may find the terms specific enough to capitalize: She went *back East* for her college reunion.

Lowercase *western* in names of plants and animals: *western larch.*

Western Hemisphere Shorebird Reserve Network, WHSRN

western redcedar but *red cedar.*

westernmost (adj.)

wet exit

Wetherill, Richard (1858–1910) explored Mesa Verde and other Anasazi sites.

wetland(s)

wetsuit, drysuit (n.)

whalebone

whale watching

wheelchair

whence means "from where," as in *the land whence it came.* The expression *from whence* is redundant.

whippoorwill no hyphens; also no hyphen in *poorwill;* but **chuck-will's-widow.**

whirling disease

whirlpool, whirlwind

whiskey not *whisky,* except in the phrase: *Scotch whisky.*

White Capitalize when referring to **Anglos.**

whitefish

whiteout used of storms.

whitetail (n.) when referring to a *white-tailed deer; whitetail buck* or *doe* also acceptable.

white-tailed (adj.) as in *white-tailed deer, white-tailed prairie dog.*

whitewater (n., adj.) not *white-water* or *white water.*

wholistic a misspelling for **holistic.**

wickiup American Indian hut covered in brush or bark mats; term usually used for dwellings in the Great Basin area. Also see **wigwam.**

-wide Compounds ending in *wide* are generally written as one word: *countywide, nationwide, statewide.*

wide-angle (adj.) a *wide-angle* lens.

Wiggler Capitalize; brand name of lures. Capitalize names of all lures of this brand, such as *Spinning Wiggler.*

wigwam Similar in construction to a **wickiup,** but used of dwellings in the Northeast.

Wild and Scenic Rivers System These rivers are managed by different agencies—some by the National Park Service, others by the U.S. Fish and Wildlife Service, the BLM, and other agencies. In most contexts, it is acceptable to refer to the river by its basic name: *the Rio Grande;* not *the Rio Grande Wild and Scenic River* unless referring specifically to its status as an entity managed under the Wild and Scenic Rivers System. To avoid ambiguity, capitalize this designation when it stands alone: The Kern River is a *Wild and Scenic River.* The river has been designated *Wild and Scenic.* Lowercase when the terms are used descriptively: this river is beautiful, wild, and scenic.

Wild Horse and Burro Program a BLM program managed under the **Wild Free-Roaming Horse and Burro Act.**

wilderness land set aside to remain pristine according to the 1964 **Wilderness Act.** Capitalize when part of a proper name: *the Desolation Wilderness, the Bob Marshall Wilderness.* The plural is *wilderness areas,* not *wildernesses.*

Wilderness Act of 1964

wilderness study area, WSA

wildflower not *wild flower.*

wildlands

wildlife (n.) usually singular.

wildlife refuge capitalize when part of a proper name: *Teller Wildlife Refuge,* the *Teller Refuge,* but *the wildlife refuge, the refuge.*

Wildlife Services formerly *Animal Damage Control (ADC).* Wildlife Services is part of the U.S. Department of Agriculture's Animal and Plant Health Inspection Service.

wildlife viewing

wildlife watcher

Wild West

wind *headwind, tailwind,* but *trade wind.* Names of winds are lowercase, except for words that are proper names: *chinook, Santa Ana.*

windblock generally; *Windbloc* is a trademark of Malden Mills, the manufacturer of Polarfleece.

windblown (adj.)

Windbreaker a brand name, though often used generically. A generic term like *windproof shell* is preferred.

windburn (n.), **windburned** (adj.)

wind chill factor no hyphen.

windfall anything (usually trees or brush) blown down by the wind. See **deadfall.**

wind gap (n.) like a **water gap,** but with no stream running through it.

windpack (n.) packed snow.

windproof (adj.)

Windstopper a trademark of W. L. Gore & Associates, Inc.

Windsurfer, Windsurfing trade names, so must be capitalized. The generic terms **sailboarder, sailboarding** are preferred.

windswept (adj.)

Winnebago, Winnebagos

Winnie-the-Pooh the fictional bear has hyphens in his name.

winterkill (n., v.)

Winter Olympics See **Olympics**.

winter over (v.) or **overwinter**

wintertime

wiregrass

-wise Avoid the use of this suffix to coin new words.

wolf, wolves, pup

wolverine, wolverines, kit

woodland(s) Lowercase as a general, descriptive term.
Capitalize *Woodland* when referring to a stage of Indian culture of the eastern United States.

woodchuck or **groundhog**, see **marmot**

Woods Hole Oceanographic Institution

woodstove

Woodsy Owl

woolly not *wooly.*

Works Progress Administration, Work Projects Administration The **WPA** began in 1935 as the *Works Progress Administration.* In 1939 the name was changed to *Work Projects Administration.*
The WPA Writers' Program produced a series of guidebooks. When citing individual WPA titles, use the name of the agency that was in use at the time of publication.

world-class (adj.)

World Cup skiing or soccer.

world-famous (adj.)

World Heritage List maintained by UNESCO. Handle as

an award, and capitalize: *Yellowstone National Park is a World Heritage site.*

Worldloppet system of marathon cross-country ski races held in different countries around the world. Not *World Loppet.* The American race is called the *American Birkebeiner.*

World Wide Web Also see **website.**

-wort Plant names that end in *wort* are generally written as one word: *saltwort, sandwort.*

would have not *would of,* as in "He *would have* reached the summit if he had started earlier."

wristband

wrist leash or **wrist loop** used to attach an ice ax.

WSA, wilderness study area

Wulff series of flies named for Lee Wulff.

XYZ

XC or **X-C** Use **cross-country** instead.

Xerox a trademark; use *photocopy* instead.

X Games sponsored by ESPN.

X-ray

Yaak, Yaak River (Montana)

yard *back yard, barn yard, rail yard.*

yaupon a plant.

yeah not *yea,* in quoted speech when the meaning is "yes."

year In ages: a *three-year-old* tent; that tent is *three years old;* a group of *ten-year-olds.* For more on ages and dates, see **Numbers,** p. 27.

> Usage note: *years' experience* or *years of experience.*

yearlong (adj.)

year-round (adj.)

yellow jacket

yellow pages lowercase.

Yellowstone cutthroat *cutts* acceptable on second reference.

yesteryear (n., adv.)

Y intersection

Yosemite Decimal System the system that rates climbing routes in the form *5.8, 5.12d,* and so on. For a detailed discussion, see *Mountaineering: The Freedom of the Hills,* listed in **For further reference.**

Yosemite National Park, Yosemite Valley

young-of-the-year animals that were born in the current year, as contrasted with *yearlings* or *two-year-olds*.

youth hostel

yo-yo (n., v.), **yo-yos** (pl.) The climber *yo-yoed* off the cliff.

Yukon Territory; the Yukon

Yunque, El peak in Luquillo Mountains, Puerto Rico.

yurt a Mongolian tent.

zero spell out. See **temperatures**.

zigzag (n., adj., adv., v.) not *zig-zag*.

Ziolkowski, Korczak (1908–1982) sculptor of the Crazy Horse monument in the Black Hills of South Dakota.

Zion Canyon, Zion National Park Note the en dash in *Zion–Mount Carmel Highway*.

ZIP code

zip-locked bag not *zip-lock* or the trade name *Ziploc*. Other generic terms: *resealable* or *self-sealing plastic bag*.

zipper fall (n.)

zone Lowercase in the phrase *time zone*. Capitalize in some place names: *Canal Zone* (Panama). Also capitalize in names of **life zones**: *Lower Sonoran Life Zone*.

zoom lens

Zuni, Zunis not *Zuñi, Zuñis* except when the alternate spelling appears in a cited book title or in quoted material. Place names: *Zuni River, Zuni Mountains*.

Appendix A:
National parks, monuments, and other federally administered areas

This appendix includes national parks, monuments, preserves, historic sites, historical parks, battlefields, and recreation areas. National trails are listed at the end of this appendix. Not included are sites that are still under development or not open to the public; affiliated areas; and sites in Washington, D.C., managed by the National Park Service.

Alabama

Horseshoe Bend National Military Park
Little River Canyon National Preserve
Russell Cave National Monument
Tuskegee Institute National Historic Site

Alaska

Aniakchak National Monument and National Preserve
Bering Land Bridge National Preserve
Cape Krusenstern National Monument
Denali National Park and National Preserve
Gates of the Arctic National Park and National
 Preserve
Glacier Bay National Park and National Preserve
Katmai National Park and National Preserve
Kenai Fjords National Park

Klondike Gold Rush National Historical Park (also
   Washington)
Kobuk Valley National Park
Lake Clark National Park and National Preserve
Noatak National Preserve
Sitka National Historical Park
Wrangell-St. Elias National Park and National Preserve
Yukon-Charley Rivers National Preserve

Arizona

Canyon de Chelly National Monument
Casa Grande Ruins National Monument
Chiricahua National Monument
Coronado National Memorial
Fort Bowie National Historic Site
Glen Canyon National Recreation Area (also Utah)
Grand Canyon National Park
Hubbell Trading Post National Historic Site
Lake Mead National Recreation Area (also Nevada)
Montezuma Castle National Monument
Navajo National Monument
Organ Pipe Cactus National Monument
Petrified Forest National Park
Pipe Spring National Monument
Saguaro National Park
Sunset Crater Volcano National Monument
Tonto National Monument
Tumacacori National Historical Park
Tuzigoot National Monument
Walnut Canyon National Monument
Wupatki National Monument

Arkansas

Arkansas Post National Memorial
Fort Smith National Historic Site (also Oklahoma)
Hot Springs National Park
Pea Ridge National Military Park

California

Cabrillo National Monument
Channel Islands National Park
Death Valley National Park (also Nevada)
Devils Postpile National Monument
Eugene O'Neill National Historic Site
Fort Point National Historic Site
Golden Gate National Recreation Area
John Muir National Historic Site
Joshua Tree National Park
Kings Canyon National Park
Lassen Volcanic National Park
Lava Beds National Monument
Manzanar National Historic Site
Mojave National Preserve
Muir Woods National Monument
Pinnacles National Monument
Point Reyes National Seashore
Redwood National Park
San Francisco Maritime National Historical Park
Santa Monica Mountains National Recreation Area
Sequoia National Park
Whiskeytown-Shasta-Trinity National Recreation Area
Yosemite National Park

Colorado

Bent's Old Fort National Historic Site
Black Canyon of the Gunnison National Monument
Colorado National Monument
Curecanti National Recreation Area
Dinosaur National Monument (also Utah)
Florissant Fossil Beds National Monument
Great Sand Dunes National Monument
Hovenweep National Monument (also Utah)
Mesa Verde National Park
Rocky Mountain National Park

Connecticut

Weir Farm National Historic Site

Florida

Big Cypress National Preserve
Biscayne National Park
Canaveral National Seashore
Castillo de San Marcos National Monument
De Soto National Memorial
Dry Tortugas National Park
Everglades National Park
Fort Caroline National Memorial
Fort Matanzas National Monument
Gulf Islands National Seashore (also Mississippi)
Timucuan Ecological and Historic Preserve

Georgia

Andersonville National Historic Site
Chattahoochee River National Recreation Area
Chickamauga and Chattanooga National Military Park
    (also Tennessee)
Cumberland Island National Seashore
Fort Frederica National Monument
Fort Pulaski National Monument
Jimmy Carter National Historic Site
Kennesaw Mountain National Battlefield Park
Martin Luther King, Jr., National Historic Site
Ocmulgee National Monument

Hawaii

Haleakala National Park
Hawaii Volcanoes National Park
Kalaupapa National Historical Park
Kaloko-Honokohau National Historical Park
Pu'uhonua o Honaunau National Historical Park
Puukohola Heiau National Historic Site
USS Arizona Memorial

Idaho

City of Rocks National Reserve
Craters of the Moon National Monument
Hagerman Fossil Beds National Monument
Nez Perce National Historical Park (also Montana, Oregon, and Washington)
Yellowstone National Park (also Montana and Wyoming)

Illinois

Lincoln Home National Historic Site

Indiana

George Rogers Clark National Historical Park
Indiana Dunes National Lakeshore
Lincoln Boyhood National Memorial

Iowa

Effigy Mounds National Monument
Herbert Hoover National Historic Site

Kansas

Fort Larned National Historic Site
Fort Scott National Historic Site

Kentucky

Abraham Lincoln Birthplace National Historic Site
Big South Fork National River and Recreation Area (also Tennessee)
Cumberland Gap National Historical Park (also Tennessee and Virginia)
Mammoth Cave National Park

Louisiana

Cane River Creole National Historical Park
Jean Lafitte National Historical Park and Preserve

Poverty Point National Monument (managed by state
of Louisiana)

Vicksburg National Military Park (also Mississippi)

Maine

Acadia National Park

Saint Croix Island International Historic Site

Maryland

Antietam National Battlefield

Assateague Island National Seashore (also Virginia)

Catoctin Mountain Park

Chesapeake and Ohio Canal National Historical Park
(also Washington, D.C., and West Virginia)

Clara Barton National Historic Site

Fort McHenry National Monument and Historic
Shrine

Fort Washington Park

Greenbelt Park

Hampton National Historic Site

Harpers Ferry National Historical Park (also Virginia
and West Virginia)

Monocacy National Battlefield

Piscataway Park

Thomas Stone National Historic Site

Massachusetts

Adams National Historic Site

Boston African American National Historic Site

Boston Harbor Islands National Recreation Area

Boston National Historical Park

Cape Cod National Seashore

Frederick Law Olmsted National Historic Site

John Fitzgerald Kennedy National Historic Site

Longfellow National Historic Site

Lowell National Historical Park

Minute Man National Historical Park

New Bedford Whaling National Historical Park
Salem Maritime National Historic Site
Saugus Iron Works National Historic Site
Springfield Armory National Historic Site

Michigan

Isle Royale National Park
Pictured Rocks National Lakeshore
Sleeping Bear Dunes National Lakeshore

Minnesota

Grand Portage National Monument
Mississippi National River and Recreation Area
Pipestone National Monument
Saint Croix National Scenic Riverway (also Wisconsin)
Voyageurs National Park

Mississippi

Brices Cross Roads National Battlefield Site
Gulf Islands National Seashore (also Florida)
Natchez National Historical Park
Tupelo National Battlefield
Vicksburg National Military Park (also Louisiana)

Missouri

George Washington Carver National Monument
Harry S Truman National Historic Site
Jefferson National Expansion Memorial
Ozark National Scenic Riverways
Ulysses S. Grant National Historic Site
Wilson's Creek National Battlefield

Montana

Big Hole National Battlefield
Bighorn Canyon National Recreation Area (also
   Wyoming)

Fort Union Trading Post National Historic Site (also
   North Dakota)
Glacier National Park
Grant-Kohrs Ranch National Historic Site
Little Bighorn Battlefield National Monument
Nez Perce National Historical Park (also Idaho,
   Oregon, and Washington)
Yellowstone National Park (also Idaho and Wyoming)

Nebraska

Agate Fossil Beds National Monument
Homestead National Monument of America
Missouri National Recreational River (also South
   Dakota)
Niobrara National Scenic Riverway
Scotts Bluff National Monument

Nevada

Death Valley National Park (also California)
Great Basin National Park
Lake Mead National Recreation Area (also Arizona)

New Hampshire

Saint-Gaudens National Historic Site

New Jersey

Delaware Water Gap National Recreation Area (also
   Pennsylvania)
Edison National Historic Site
Gateway National Recreation Area (also New York)
Great Egg Harbor Scenic and Recreational River
Middle Delaware National Scenic River (also
   Pennsylvania)
Morristown National Historical Park
Statue of Liberty National Monument (also New York)

New Mexico

Aztec Ruins National Monument
Bandelier National Monument
Capulin Volcano National Monument
Carlsbad Caverns National Park
Chaco Culture National Historical Park
El Malpais National Monument
El Morro National Monument
Fort Union National Monument
Gila Cliff Dwellings National Monument
Pecos National Historical Park
Petroglyph National Monument
Salinas Pueblo Missions National Monument
White Sands National Monument

New York

Castle Clinton National Monument
Eleanor Roosevelt National Historic Site
Federal Hall National Memorial
Fire Island National Seashore
Fort Stanwix National Monument
Gateway National Recreation Area (also New Jersey)
General Grant National Memorial
Home of Franklin D. Roosevelt National Historic Site
Martin Van Buren National Historic Site
Sagamore Hill National Historic Site
Saint Paul's Church National Historic Site
Saratoga National Historical Park
Statue of Liberty National Monument (also New
    Jersey)
Theodore Roosevelt Birthplace National Historic Site
Theodore Roosevelt Inaugural National Historic Site
Upper Delaware Scenic and Recreational River (also
    Pennsylvania)
Vanderbilt Mansion National Historic Site
Women's Rights National Historical Park

North Carolina

Cape Hatteras National Seashore
Cape Lookout National Seashore
Carl Sandburg Home National Historic Site
Fort Raleigh National Historic Site
Great Smoky Mountains National Park (also
   Tennessee)
Guilford Courthouse National Military Park
Moores Creek National Battlefield
Wright Brothers National Memorial

North Dakota

Fort Union Trading Post National Historic Site (also
   Montana)
Knife River Indian Villages National Historic Site
Theodore Roosevelt National Park

Ohio

Cuyahoga Valley National Recreation Area
Dayton Aviation Heritage National Historical Park
Hopewell Culture National Historical Park
James A. Garfield National Historic Site
Perry's Victory and International Peace Memorial
William Howard Taft National Historic Site

Oklahoma

Chickasaw National Recreation Area
Fort Smith National Historic Site (also Arkansas)
Washita Battlefield National Historic Site

Oregon

Crater Lake National Park
Fort Clatsop National Memorial
John Day Fossil Beds National Monument
Nez Perce National Historical Park (also Idaho,
   Montana, and Washington)

Pennsylvania

Allegheny Portage Railroad National Historic Site
Delaware Water Gap National Recreation Area (also New Jersey)
Edgar Allan Poe National Historic Site
Eisenhower National Historic Site
Fort Necessity National Battlefield
Friendship Hill National Historic Site
Gettysburg National Military Park
Hopewell Furnace National Historic Site
Independence National Historical Park
Johnstown Flood National Memorial
Middle Delaware National Scenic River (also New Jersey)
Steamtown National Historic Site
Thaddeus Kosciuszko National Memorial
Upper Delaware Scenic and Recreational River (also New York)
Valley Forge National Historical Park

Rhode Island

Roger Williams National Memorial

South Carolina

Charles Pinckney National Historic Site
Congaree Swamp National Monument
Cowpens National Battlefield
Fort Sumter National Monument
Kings Mountain National Military Park
Ninety Six National Historic Site

South Dakota

Badlands National Park
Jewel Cave National Monument
Missouri National Recreational River (also Nebraska)
Mount Rushmore National Memorial
Wind Cave National Park

Tennessee

Andrew Johnson National Historic Site
Big South Fork National River and Recreation Area
    (also Kentucky)
Chickamauga and Chattanooga National Military Park
    (also Georgia)
Cumberland Gap National Historical Park (also
    Kentucky and Virginia)
Fort Donelson National Battlefield
Great Smoky Mountains National Park (also North
    Carolina)
Shiloh National Military Park
Stones River National Battlefield

Texas

Alibates Flint Quarries National Monument
Amistad National Recreation Area
Big Bend National Park
Big Thicket National Preserve
Chamizal National Memorial
Fort Davis National Historic Site
Guadalupe Mountains National Park
Lake Meredith National Recreation Area
Lyndon B. Johnson National Historical Park
Padre Island National Seashore
Palo Alto Battlefield National Historic Site
San Antonio Missions National Historical Park

Utah

Arches National Park
Bryce Canyon National Park
Canyonlands National Park
Capitol Reef National Park
Cedar Breaks National Monument
Dinosaur National Monument (also Colorado)
Grand Staircase–Escalante National Monument
    (managed by BLM)

Glen Canyon National Recreation Area (also Arizona)
Golden Spike National Historic Site
Hovenweep National Monument (also Colorado)
Natural Bridges National Monument
Rainbow Bridge National Monument
Timpanogos Cave National Monument
Zion National Park

Vermont

Marsh-Billings National Historical Park

Virginia

Appomattox Court House National Historical Park
Arlington House, Robert E. Lee Memorial
Assateague Island National Seashore (also Maryland)
Booker T. Washington National Monument
Colonial National Historical Park
Cumberland Gap National Historical Park (also
    Kentucky and Tennessee)
Fredericksburg and Spotsylvania County Battlefields
    Memorial National Military Park
George Washington Birthplace National Monument
Harpers Ferry National Historical Park (also Maryland
    and West Virginia)
Maggie L. Walker National Historic Site
Manassas National Battlefield Park
Petersburg National Battlefield
Prince William Forest Park
Richmond National Battlefield Park
Shenandoah National Park
Wolf Trap Farm Park for the Performing Arts

Washington

Ebey's Landing National Historical Reserve
Fort Vancouver National Historic Site
Klondike Gold Rush National Historical Park (also
    Alaska)

Lake Chelan National Recreation Area
Lake Roosevelt National Recreation Area
Mount Rainier National Park
Nez Perce National Historical Park (also Idaho, Oregon, and Montana)
North Cascades National Park
Olympic National Park
Ross Lake National Recreation Area
San Juan Island National Historical Park
Whitman Mission National Historic Site

West Virginia

Chesapeake and Ohio Canal National Historical Park (also Maryland and Washington, D.C.)
Gauley River National Recreation Area
Harpers Ferry National Historical Park (also Maryland and Virginia)
New River Gorge National River

Wisconsin

Apostle Islands National Lakeshore
Saint Croix National Scenic Riverway (also Minnesota)

Wyoming

Bighorn Canyon National Recreation Area (also Montana)
Devils Tower National Monument
Fort Laramie National Historic Site
Fossil Butte National Monument
Grand Teton National Park
Yellowstone National Park (also Idaho and Montana)

Territories

American Samoa

National Park of American Samoa

Guam

War in the Pacific National Historical Park

Puerto Rico

San Juan National Historic Site

Virgin Islands

Buck Island Reef National Monument
Christiansted National Historic Site
Salt River Bay National Historical Park and Ecological
    Preserve
Virgin Islands National Park

National trails

Appalachian National Scenic Trail
California National Historic Trail
Continental Divide National Scenic Trail
Florida National Scenic Trail
Ice Age National Scenic Trail
Iditarod National Historic Trail
Juan Bautista de Anza National Historic Trail
Lewis and Clark National Historic Trail
Mormon Pioneer National Historic Trail
Natchez Trace National Scenic Trail
Nez Perce National Historic Trail
North Country National Scenic Trail
Oregon National Historic Trail
Overmountain Victory National Historic Trail
Pacific Crest National Scenic Trail
Pony Express National Historic Trail
Potomac Heritage National Scenic Trail
Santa Fe National Historic Trail
Selma to Montgomery National Historic Trail
Trail of Tears National Historic Trail

Appendix B:
Indian tribes

Although *Indian, American Indian,* and *Native American* are all
acceptable terms, use of specific tribal names is preferred. The
following list suggests preferred spellings for many tribal names,
with annotations when the name of a specific tribal entity differs
from the most common spelling. In most cases, form the plural
simply by adding the letter "s": two *Navajos.* This may result in an
awkward form, as when the name of the tribe ends in "s"; such
names should be handled on a case-by-case basis. When speaking
of people as a cultural group, not as individuals, usually use the
singular form (the *Navajo,* like the *French*), although this is sometimes a matter of sound.

Most of the terms included here appear in the names of tribal
entities recognized by the Bureau of Indian Affairs.

A complete list of federally recognized tribal entities, including
Alaska Native villages, may be found at the Bureau of Indian
Affairs (BIA) website, www.doi.gov/bureau-indian-affairs.html.

For another source of spellings of Indian tribal names, see the
Library of Congress subject headings under "Indians of North
America." However, many of these spellings differ from the
spellings of the tribal entities as recognized by the BIA.

Pueblos of the Rio Grande are listed under Pueblo. Entries for
prehistoric Indian cultures (such as Anasazi or Ancestral Puebloan)
are found in the main section of this book.

Appendix B: Indian tribes

Apache

Arapaho
  *but Arapahoe Tribe of the Wind
  River Reservation, Wyoming*

Assiniboine

Bannock

Blackfeet
  *Blackfeet Tribe of the Blackfeet
  Indian Reservation of Montana*
  *Blackfoot only when referring to the
  Blackfoot Confederacy*

Caddo

Cahuilla

Catawba

Cayuga

Chemehuevi

Cherokee

Cheyenne

Chickasaw

Chippewa

Chitimacha

Choctaw

Chukchansi

Chumash

Cocopah

Coeur D'Alene

Colville

Comanche

Coos

Coquille

Coushatta

Cree

Creek

Crow

Dakota

Delaware

Diegueño

Elwha

Gila

Goshute not Gosiute

Grand Ronde

Havasupai

Hidatsa

Ho-Chunk Nation of
  Wisconsin (formerly
  Wisconsin Winnebago
  Tribe)

Hoh

Hoopa not Hupa

Hopi

Hualapai

Hunkpapa

Iroquois

Kalispel *not Kalispell, the town in Montana*

Karuk *not Karok*

Kaw

Kickapoo

Kiowa

Klamath

Kootenai *not Kutenai*

Luiseño

Lummi

Maidu

Makah

Maliseet *not Malecite*

Mandan

Maricopa

Mechoopda

Menominee

Me-Wuk *see Miwok*

Miami

Miccosukee *not Mikasuki*

Miniconjou

Miwok *not Me-Wuk*
but if mentioning a specific tribal entity, use the spelling of that group's name: Ione Band of Miwok Indians of California, but Jackson Rancheria of Me-Wuk Indians of California.

Modoc

Mohave/Mojave
Fort McDowell Mohave-Apache Community of the Fort McDowell Indian Reservation, Arizona; Fort Mojave Indian Tribe of Arizona, California and Nevada

Mohawk

Mohegan

Mohican

Mono

Muckleshoot

Muscogee

Narragansett

Navajo Nation *not Navaho*

Nez Perce

Nisqually

Nomlaki

Nooksack

Odawa

Oglala

Omaha

Oneida

Onondaga

Osage

Oto
but Otoe-Missouria Tribe of Indians, Oklahoma

Appendix B: Indian tribes

Ottawa

Paiute

Passamaquoddy

Pawnee

Penobscot

Peoria

Pequot

Pima

Pit River

Pomo

Ponca

Potawatomi/Potawatomie
*Potawatomi except in the name of
the Hannahville Indian
Community of Wisconsin
Potawatomie Indians of Michigan.*

Pueblos of the Rio Grande:
*Acoma
Cochiti
Jemez
Isleta
Laguna
Nambe
Picuris
Pojoaque
San Felipe
San Juan
San Ildefonso
Sandia
Santa Ana
Santa Clara*

*Santo Domingo
Taos
Tesuque
Zia*

Puyallup

Quapaw

Quechan

Quileute

Quinault

Quinnipiac

Sac & Fox

Salish *not Flathead*
*Confederated Salish and Kootenai
Tribes of the Flathead Reservation,
Montana*

Samish

Sans Arc

Santee

Sauk-Suiattle

Seminole

Seneca

Serrano

Shawnee

Shoshone/Shoshoni
*Shoshone except in the name of the
Northwestern Band of Shoshoni
Nation of Utah (Washakie).*

Sinkyone

Sioux

Siuslaw

Skagit

S'Klallam

Skokomish

Sokoki

Spokane

Squaxin Island

Stillaguamish

Suquamish

Swinomish

Tohono O'odham

Tonkawa

Tulalip

Tule River

Tunica-Biloxi

Tuscarora

Umatilla

Umpqua

Ute

Wailaki

Wampanoag

Warm Springs

Washoe *not Washo*

Wichita

Winnebago

Winnemucca

Wintun

Wiyot

Wyandotte *not Wyandot*

Yakama *not Yakima*

Yankton

Yaqui

Yavapai

Yokuts

Ysleta Del Sur

Yurok

Zuni

Appendix C:
Federal departments and agencies

Bureau of Indian Affairs (BIA)
Public Affairs Office
1849 C Street NW
Washington, DC 20240
202-208-3710
www.doi.gov/bureau-indian-affairs.html

Bureau of Land Management (BLM)
Office of Public Affairs
1849 C Street Room LS-406
Washington, DC 20240
202-452-5125
www.blm.gov

Bureau of Reclamation (USBR or BuRec)
Public Affairs Division
1849 C Street NW
Washington, DC 20240
202-208-4662
www.usbr.gov/main/index.html

Environmental Protection Agency (EPA)
401 M Street SW
Washington, DC 20460
202-260-2090
www.epa.gov

USDA Forest Service (USDAFS)

Office of Communications
P.O. Box 96090
Washington, DC 20090-6090
202-205-8333
www.fs.fed.us

Department of the Interior

1849 C Street NW
Washington, DC 20240
202-208-3171
www.doi.gov

Minerals Management Service (MMS)

Office of Communications
1849 C Street NW
Washington, DC 20240
202-208-3985
www.mms.gov

National Marine Fisheries Service (NMFS)

1315 East-West Highway
Silver Spring, MD 20910
301-713-2239
kingfish.ssp.nmfs.gov

National Oceanic and Atmospheric Administration (NOAA)

Department of Commerce
Washington, DC 20230
202-482-2985
www.noaa.gov

National Ocean Service (NOS)

Room 13632
1305 East-West Highway
Silver Spring, MD 20910
301-713-3074
www.nos.noaa.gov

National Park Service (NPS)

Office of Public Affairs
P.O. Box 37127
Washington, DC 20013-7127
202-208-6843
www.nps.gov

National Weather Service (NWS)

1325 East-West Highway
Silver Spring, MD 20910-3283
301-713-0689
www.nws.noaa.gov

Natural Resources Conservation Service (NRCS)

Department of Agriculture
P.O. Box 2890
Washington, DC 20013
202-690-4811

Office of Surface Mining Reclamation and Enforcement (OSMRE)

Office of Communications
Department of the Interior
Washington, DC 20240
202-208-2719
www.osmre.gov/osm.htm

U.S. Army Corps of Engineers (USACE)

20 Massachusetts Avenue NW
Washington, DC 20314
202-761-0660
www.usace.army.mil

U.S. Fish and Wildlife Service (USFWS)

Office of Public Affairs
Department of the Interior
Washington, DC 20240
202-208-5634
www.fws.gov

U.S. Geological Survey (USGS)

Eastern Region and Headquarters:

USGS National Center
12201 Sunrise Valley Drive
Reston, VA 20192
703-648-4000

Central Region:

U.S. Geological Survey
Box 25046 Denver Federal Center
Denver, CO 80225
303-236-5900

Western Region:

U.S. Geological Survey
345 Middlefield Road
Menlo Park, CA 94025
650-853-8300
www.usgs.gov
1-888-ASK-USGS (1-888-275-8747)

The U.S. Department of Agriculture includes the USDA Forest Service and the Natural Resources Conservation Service (formerly the Soil Conservation Service).

The Department of Commerce includes the National Oceanic and Atmospheric Administration (NOAA). NOAA includes the National Marine Fisheries Service, National Ocean Service, and National Weather Service.

The Department of the Interior includes the following agencies: Bureau of Indian Affairs; Bureau of Land Management; Bureau of Reclamation; Minerals Management Service; National Park Service; Office of Surface Mining Reclamation and Enforcement; U.S. Fish and Wildlife Service; U.S. Geological Survey.

Appendix D:
State departments and agencies

An Internet address of the form www.state.xx.us, where xx is
the postal abbreviation for the state, brings you to the state's
website, from which you can access that state's departments
and agencies.

Alabama

>   Department of Conservation and Natural Resources
>   Division of Game and Fish
>   Division of Parks

Alaska

>   Department of Fish and Game
>   Department of Natural Resources
>   Division of Parks and Outdoor Recreation

Arizona

>   Game & Fish Department
>   Arizona State Parks

Arkansas

>   Game & Fish Commission
>   Department of Parks and Tourism

California

>   Department of Fish and Game
>   Department of Parks and Recreation

Colorado

Department of Natural Resources
Division of Wildlife
Division of State Parks and Outdoor Recreation

Connecticut

Bureau of Fisheries and Wildlife
Department of Environmental Protection

Delaware

Department of Natural Resources and Environmental
Control
Division of Fish & Wildlife
Division of Parks and Recreation

District of Columbia

Department of Consumer and Regulatory Affairs,
Fisheries, and Management Branch
Department of Recreation and Parks; also National
Park Service

Florida

Game and Fresh Water Fish Commission
Department of Environmental Protection
Division of Recreation and Parks

Georgia

Department of Natural Resources
Wildlife Resources Division
Parks, Recreation and Historic Sites Division

Hawaii

Department of Land and Natural Resources
Division of Aquatic Resources
Division of Forestry and Wildlife
Division of State Parks

Idaho

Fish and Game Department
Department of Parks and Recreation

Illinois

Department of Natural Resources

Indiana

Department of Natural Resources
Division of Fish & Wildlife
Division of State Parks & Reservoirs
Division of Outdoor Recreation

Iowa

Department of Natural Resources
Fish and Wildlife Division
Division of Parks, Recreation and Preserves

Kansas

Department of Wildlife & Parks

Kentucky

Department of Fish and Wildlife Resources
Department of Parks

Louisiana

Department of Wildlife and Fisheries
Department of Natural Resources
Department of Culture, Recreation & Tourism, Office
of State Parks

Maine

Department of Inland Fisheries & Wildlife
Department of Conservation, Bureau of Parks and
Recreation

Maryland

Department of Natural Resources
Fisheries Service
Forest, Wildlife and Heritage Service
State Forest and Park Service

Massachusetts

Department of Fisheries & Wildlife
Department of Environmental Management, Division
of Forests and Parks

Michigan

Department of Natural Resources
Fisheries Division
Wildlife Division
Parks and Recreation Division

Minnesota

Department of Natural Resources
Division of Fish and Wildlife
Division of Parks and Recreation

Mississippi

Department of Wildlife, Fisheries and Parks

Missouri

Department of Conservation
Department of Natural Resources, Division of State
Parks

Montana

Department of Fish, Wildlife & Parks

Nebraska

Game and Parks Commission

Nevada

Department of Conservation and Natural Resources
Division of Wildlife
Division of State Parks

New Hampshire

Fish and Game Department
Department of Resources & Economic Development,
   Division of Parks and Recreation

New Jersey

Division of Fish, Game and Wildlife
Division of Parks and Forestry

New Mexico

Department of Game and Fish
Park and Recreation Division

New York

Department of Environmental Conservation, Division
   of Fish, Wildlife, and Marine Resources
Office of Parks, Recreation and Historic Preservation

North Carolina

Wildlife Resources Commission
Department of Environment and Natural Resources,
   Division of Parks and Recreation

North Dakota

Game and Fish Department
Parks & Recreation Department

Ohio

Department of Natural Resources
Division of Wildlife
Division of Parks and Recreation

Division of Natural Areas and Preserves

Oklahoma

Department of Wildlife Conservation
Tourism & Recreation Department

Oregon

Department of Fish and Wildlife
Parks and Recreation Department

Pennsylvania

Game Commission
Fish and Boat Commission
Department of Environmental Resources, Bureau of
State Parks

Rhode Island

Department of Environmental Management
Division of Fish, Wildlife and Estuarine Resources
Division of Parks and Recreation

South Carolina

Department of Natural Resources
Division of Wildlife & Marine Resources
Department of Parks, Recreation and Tourism

South Dakota

Department of Game, Fish and Parks
Division of Wildlife
Division of Parks and Recreation

Tennessee

Wildlife Resources Agency
Department of Environment and Conservation
Division of Natural Heritage

Texas

Parks and Wildlife Department

Utah

Department of Natural Resources
Division of Wildlife Resources
Division of State Parks and Recreation

Vermont

Department of Fish and Wildlife
Department of Forests, Parks & Recreation

Virginia

Department of Game and Inland Fisheries
Department of Conservation & Recreation

Washington

Department of Fish and Wildlife
State Parks and Recreation Commission

West Virginia

Department of Natural Resources
Division of Wildlife Resources
Division of Tourism and Parks

Wisconsin

Department of Natural Resources
Bureau of Parks and Recreation

Wyoming

Game and Fish Department
Department of Commerce, Division of Parks and
Cultural Resources

Appendix E:
Outdoor clubs and organizations

This list includes conservation and sports organizations and coalitions, professional organizations, field schools, and events. Most are national; a few are regional.

Access Fund

Adirondack Mountain Club (ADK)

Alpine Club of Canada (ACC)

American Alpine Club (AAC)

American Birding Association (ABA)

American Canoe Association (ACA)

American Cetacean Society (ACS)

The American Forestry Association (AFA)—The always capitalized.

American Forests

American Fraternal Snowshoe Union (part of International Snowshoe Association)

American Hiking Society (AHS)

American Horticultural Society (AHS)

American Humane Society (AHS)

American Mountain Guides Association (AMGA)

American Ornithologists' Union (AOU)

American Rivers (no acronym)

American Rock Art Research Association (ARARA)

American Whitewater Affiliation (AWA)

American Wilderness Alliance

Appalachian Mountain Club (AMC)

Appalachian Trail Conference (ATC)

The Archaeological Conservancy

Archaeological Institute of America (AIA)

Audubon—See National Audubon Society,
    Massachusetts Audubon Society

Banff Mountain Film Festival

Bass Anglers Sportsman Society (BASS)

Bat Conservation International (BCI)

Boone & Crockett Club (B&C)

Canadian Snowshoe Association (part of International
    Snowshoe Association)

Canyonlands Field Institute (CFI)

Crow Canyon Archaeological Center

Defenders of Wildlife—not the Defenders of Wildlife;
    no acronym; Defenders in subsequent references.

Desert Survivors

Desert Tortoise Council

Ducks Unlimited (DU)

Earth Island Institute

Earth First!

Elderhostel (no abbreviation)

Fish Unlimited

Foundation of North American Wild Sheep (FNAWS)

Four Corners School of Outdoor Education

Friends of the Earth

Friends of the River

Friends of the Sea Otter (FSO)

Future Fisherman Foundation (FFF)

Glacier Institute

Grand Canyon Trust

Great Bear Foundation (GBF)

Greater Yellowstone Coalition (GYC)

International Association of Fish and Wildlife Agencies (IAFWA)

International Federation of Environmental Journalists (IFEJ)

International Game Fish Association (IGFA)

International Mountain Bicycling Association (IMBA)

International Rivers Network

International Snowshoe Association (comprises American Fraternal Snowshoe Union and Canadian Snowshoe Association)

Iowa Prairie Network (IPN)

The Izaak Walton League of America, Inc. (IWLA)

League of Conservation Voters (LCV)

Leave No Trace, Inc. (LNT)

Massachusetts Audubon Society (independent from National Audubon Society)

Mountain Lion Foundation (MLF)

The Mountaineers—*The* always capitalized.

National Association for Interpretation (NAI)

National Audubon Society (Audubon)

National Caves Association (NCA)

National Organization for River Sports (NORS)

National Organization of Whitewater Rodeos (NOWR)—a committee of the American Whitewater Affiliation.

National Outdoor Leadership School (NOLS)

National Paddling Film Festival (NPFF)

National Parks and Conservation Association (NPCA)

National Shooting Sports Foundation (NSSF)

National Speleological Society (NSS)

National Trust for Historic Preservation (NTHP)

National Wetlands Conservation Alliance

National Wildflower Research Center (NWRC)

National Wildlife Federation (NWF)

National Wild Turkey Federation

The Nature Conservancy (TNC)—*The* always capitalized; the Conservancy on second reference.

North American Skijoring and Ski Pulk Association (NASSPA)

North American Trail Ride Conference (NATRC)

Outdoor Writers Association of America

Outward Bound

Pacific Northwest Trail Foundation (no abbreviation)

Passport in Time (PIT)

Peregrine Fund (PF)

Pheasants Forever (no abbreviation)

Professional Disc Golf Association (PDGA)

Professional Paddlesports Association (PPA)

Public Lands Interpretive Association

Quail Unlimited (QU)

Rails-to-Trails Conservancy (RTC)

Rainforest Action Network

Rainforest Alliance (RA)

Rocky Mountain Elk Foundation (RMEF)—never the Rocky Mountain Elk Foundation.

Ruffed Grouse Society (RGS)

Safari Club International (SCI)

Salmon Unlimited (SU)

Save-the-Redwoods League (SRL)

Sierra Club (no abbreviation)—*Sierra*, alone, refers to the magazine published by the Sierra Club.

Society of Environmental Journalists (SEJ)

Southern Utah Wilderness Alliance (SUWA)

Southwest Natural and Cultural Heritage Association (SNCHA)

Southwest Parks and Monuments Association

Sport Fishing Institute (SFI)

Stripers Unlimited (SU)

Student Conservation Association (SCA)

Surfrider Foundation

Teton Science School

Trout Unlimited (TU)

Uintah Mountain Club

Union Internationale des Associations d'Alpinisme (UIAA)

United States Canoe Association (USCA)

Utah Wilderness Coalition (UWC)

Wasatch Mountain Club

Western Saddle Clubs Association, Inc. (WSCA)

Whitetails Unlimited (WU)

The Wilderness Society (TWS)

Wild Rockies Field Institute

World Monuments Watch

Yellowstone Association Institute

For Further Reference

Style guides and other general reference

American Heritage Dictionary of the English Language. 3rd ed. Boston: Houghton Mifflin Co., 1992.

The Associated Press Stylebook and Libel Manual. 6th trade ed. Ed. Norm Goldstein. Reading, Mass.: Addison-Wesley, 1996.

The Cambridge Dictionary of American Biography. Ed. John S. Bowman. Cambridge: Cambridge University Press, 1995. Includes an occupational index, so if you are not sure of the spelling, you can search for the person by occupation.

The Chicago Manual of Style. 14th ed. Chicago: University of Chicago Press, 1993.

The Elements of Style. William Strunk, Jr., and E. B. White. 3rd ed. New York: Macmillan Publishing Co., 1979. A classic, especially useful for authors and copy editors.

*For Further
Reference*

The Elements of Typographic Style. Ed. Robert Bringhurst. 2nd
ed. Vancouver, B.C.: Hartley & Marks, 1996.

The Gregg Reference Manual. William A. Sabin. 8th ed. Lake
Forest, Ill.: Glencoe/McGraw-Hill, 1996. A
grammar and punctuation guide. Sometimes easier to
use than *Chicago* (but the rules in *Chicago* always take
precedence).

*Guidelines for Reporting and Writing About People with
Disabilities.* Lawrence, Kans.: Research and Training
Center on Independent Living, 1996. This pamphlet
is a good source for appropriate terms for referring
to people with disabilities. Call the center at 913-
864-4095 for copies.

Judd, Karen. *Copyediting: A Practical Guide.* 2nd ed. Los Altos,
Calif.: Crisp Publications, 1990. Helpful for questions of hyphenation and handling of numbers.

Merriam-Webster's Biographical Dictionary. Springfield, Mass.:
Merriam-Webster, Inc., 1995.

Merriam-Webster's Collegiate Dictionary. 10th ed. Springfield,
Mass.: Merriam-Webster, Inc., 1997.

The New York Public Library Desk Reference. New York:
Webster's New World, 1989. A general reference,
useful on a wide range of topics.

Skillin, Marjorie E. *Words Into Type.* 3rd ed. Englewood Cliffs,
N.J.: Prentice-Hall, 1974.

Swan, Jennifer. *Sports Style Guide and Reference Manual.*
Chicago: Triumph Books, 1996. The subject is professional sports.

United States Government Printing Office Style Manual.
Washington, D.C.: 1984. Especially helpful for compounding and hyphenation. Includes list of counties
by state.

The World Almanac and Book of Facts. Mahwah, N.J.: Funk &
Wagnalls, latest edition. A good general reference for
facts and statistics.

Grammar and usage

Bernstein, Theodor M. *The Careful Writer: A Modern Guide to
English Usage.* New York: Atheneum, 1965.

Follett, Wilson. *Modern American Usage: A Guide.* Revised by
Erik Wensberg. New York: Hill and Wang, 1998.
Helpful on general questions of usage, but sometimes too conservative for writing about the outdoors (for example, this book objects to the coinage
of the word *permafrost*).

Hendrickson, Robert. *Happy Trails: A Dictionary of Western
Expressions.* New York: Facts on File, 1994.

Maggio, Rosalie. *The Dictionary of Bias-Free Usage: A Guide to
Nondiscriminatory Language.* Phoenix: Oryx Press,
1991. Covers alternatives to racist as well as sexist
language (suggests *single file* for *Indian file*, for
instance).

Miller, Casey, and Kate Swift. *The Handbook of Nonsexist
Writing.* 2nd ed. New York: Harper & Row, 1988.

Other reference
(listed by subject)

archaeology

Folsom, Franklin, and Mary Elting Folsom. *America's Ancient Treasures: A Guide to Archeological Sites and Museums in the United States and Canada.* 4th revised, enlarged edition. Albuquerque: University of New Mexico Press, 1993. Organized by region and state. Includes glossary of archaeological terms; directory of archaeological societies; directory of state and provincial archaeologists.

Whitehouse, Ruth D., ed. *The Facts on File Dictionary of Archaeology.* New York: Facts on File, 1983.

birds

American Ornithologists' Union (AOU). *Check-list of North American Birds, 6th ed.* Lawrence, Kans.: American Ornithologists' Union, 1983.

Cox, Randall T. *Birder's Dictionary.* Helena, Mont.: Falcon Press, 1996.

climbing and mountaineering

Child, Greg, ed. *Climbing: The Complete Reference to Rock, Ice and Indoor Climbing.* New York: Facts on File, 1995. An A-Z reference on climbing history, areas, techniques, gear, notable climbers, and more. Some typographical errors make this book a better backup reference than first source, however. Includes key to symbols and abbreviations; comparison chart of international rating systems.

Gerrard, Layne. *Rock Gear: Everybody's Guide to Rock Climbing Equipment.* Berkeley, Calif.: Ten Speed Press, 1990. A reference for information, not style. Unfortunately, the organization of this book makes it hard to use.

Graydon, Don, and Kurt Hanson, eds. *Mountaineering: The Freedom of the Hills.* 6th ed. Seattle: The Mountaineers, 1997.

companies and trade names

Brands and Their Companies. 18th ed. 2 vols. Ed. Jennifer L. Carman and Christine A. Kesler. Detroit: Gale Research, 1998.

Companies and Their Brands. 18th ed. 2 vols. Ed. Jennifer L. Carman and Christine A. Kesler. Detroit: Gale Research, 1998.

ecology

A Dictionary of Ecology. Ed. Michael Allaby. 2nd ed. Oxford: Oxford University Press, 1998.

field guides

We recommend the latest edition of the National Audubon Society series of field guides.

fishing

McClane, A. J., ed. *McClane's Standard Fishing Encyclopedia and International Angling Guide.* New York: Holt, Rinehart and Winston, 1965.

For Further
Reference

general outdoors

Sparano, Vin T. *Complete Outdoors Encyclopedia*. New York: St.
Martin's Press, 1998. A traditional sportsman's
guide (with the emphasis on *man*). Look past the
references to boxer shorts as a base clothing layer,
and you will find useful information about guns,
hunting, bowhunting, game, fishing, and boating.

geology

Dictionary of Geological Terms. Prepared by the American
Geological Institute. Robert L. Bates and Julia A.
Jackson, eds. 3rd ed. New York: Anchor Books,
1984. Entries include notes on regional usage and
synonyms.

guns and hunting

Barnes, Frank C., and M. C. McPherson. *Cartridges of the
World: A Complete and Illustrated Reference Source for
over 1500 of the World's Sporting Cartridges*. 8th ed.
Iola: Krause Publications, 1996.

The New Hunter's Encyclopedia. 3rd rev. ed. Harrisburg, Penn.:
Stackpole Books, 1966. No longer "new," but will
still tell you that as a verb, *field-dress* has a hyphen.

Jarrett, William S., ed. *Shooter's Bible*. No. 90. Wayne, N.J.:
Stoeger Publishing Co., 1999.

history

The American Heritage Encyclopedia of American History. Ed.
John Mack Faragher. New York: Henry Holt,
1998.

The New Encyclopedia of the American West. Ed. Howard R.
Lamar. New Haven: Yale University Press, 1998.

Indians

American Indian Reservations and Trust Areas. Ed. Veronica E.
Velarde Tiller. Washington, D.C.: Department of
Commerce, Economic Development
Administration, 1996. Includes federally recognized tribes, tribes that are state-recognized only,
and Alaska Native corporations. Includes contact
information.

The Bureau of Indian Affairs website, *www.doi.gov/bureau-
indian-affairs.html,* includes a list of federally recognized tribal entities (including Alaska Native
villages).

Davis, Mary B., ed. *Native America in the Twentieth Century:
An Encyclopedia.* New York: Garland Publishing,
1996. Alphabetical entries are further organized
by an index of articles by subject. Useful for
information on organizations, policies, and institu-
tions, as well as on individual tribes.

Hoxie, Frederick E., ed. *Encyclopedia of North American
Indians.* Boston: Houghton Mifflin Co., 1996.

place names

*CSG State Directory. Directory III: Administrative Officials
1998.* Lexington, Ky.: Council of State
Governments, 1998. Behind the bureaucratic title
lurks an easy to use source for names and contact
information for state government agencies, organized by function.

Dickson, Paul. *Labels for Locals: What to Call People from
Abilene to Zimbabwe.* Springfield, Mass.: Merriam-
Webster, Inc., 1997. The book to consult if you
want to know why Utahns are Utahns, not
Utahans.

Merriam-Webster's Geographical Dictionary. 3rd ed. Springfield,
Mass.: Merriam-Webster, Inc., 1997. A good reference for spelling of foreign place names.

National Five-Digit ZIP Code and Post Office Directory. 2 vols.
Washington, D.C.: United States Postal Service,
latest edition. Can be used as a first reference for
spelling of United States place names. Is there
really no hyphen in the name of the California
town, Twentynine Palms? You can confirm that
spelling here.

The National Parks: Index 1997–1999. Washington, D.C.:
National Park Service, 1997.

Schneider, Russ, ed. *The Wilderness Directory: A Quick-
Reference Guide to America's Wilderness.* Helena,
Mont.: Falcon Publishing, 1998.

The U.S. Geological Survey website, *www.usgs.gov,* includes a
geographic names database.

The United States Government Manual. Office of the Federal
Register, National Archives and Records
Administration, latest edition. Good for names
and contact information for federal agencies.
Includes an appendix of abbreviations and
acronyms.